ESSENTIAL
PERENNIALS

ESSENTIAL
PERENNIALS

The 100 Best for Design and Cultivation

Text and Photography by Derek Fell

CRESCENT BOOKS
NEW YORK

A FRIEDMAN GROUP BOOK

This 1989 edition published by Crescent Books
distributed by Crown Publishers, Inc.
225 Park Avenue South
New York, New York 10003

Library of Congress Cataloging-in-Publication Data

Essential perennials
p.   cm.—(The Essential garden planning series)

ISBN 0-517-66178-0

1. Perennials.   2. Perennials—Pictorial works.   3. Gardens-Designs and plans.
I. Series.

SB434.E77 1989   88-21733
716—dc19   CIP

ESSENTIAL PERENNIALS: The 100 Best for Design and Cultivation
was prepared and produced by
Michael Friedman Publishing Group, Inc.
15 West 26th Street
New York, New York 10010

Editor: Sharon Kalman
Art Director/Designer: Robert W. Kosturko
Layout: Devorah Levinrad
Photo Editor: Christopher Bain
Production Manager: Karen Greenberg
Illustrations: Alanna M. Georgens

Color separated, printed, and bound by
South Sea International Press, Inc.

h g f e d c b a

ACKNOWLEDGMENTS

Thanks to the many garden owners with perennial borders who kindly allowed me to photograph their plantings. Also, thanks for the many tips and planting secrets they shared.

TABLE OF CONTENTS

INTRODUCTION

FLORAL BEAUTY YEAR AFTER YEAR

A COLORFUL PERENNIAL BORDER IS A HIGHLY popular garden feature. It not only provides an old-fashioned accent, but, when properly planted, brings a sophisticated beauty to the garden that no other group of herbaceous plants can match. Not as gaudy as beds of annuals, not as short-flowering as most bulb plantings, perennials offer extensive design possibilities.

First, it's important to know what a perennial is in comparison to other groups of plants, such as *annuals*, which complete their life cycle in a year, and *biennials*, which complete their life cycle in two years. However, biennials often give the appearance of being perennials because they generally seed themselves freely, and so seedlings are always springing up in the bed to replace the older plants. Broadly defined, a perennial can be any plant that lives for more than two years, producing foliage the first year and flowering the next, then under favorable conditions, continues to flower year after year. Based on this definition, all shrubs and bulbs could be considered perennials. However, in horticultural circles true perennials are considered different from bulbs because bulbs have a unique ability to survive periods of stress—such as severe cold or drought—because of their swollen underground food store, called a bulb (also called a rhizome, corm, or tuber, depending on its composition). True perennials are also distinguished from most shrubs because shrubs develop a special, durable cell structure known as "wood." A small group of plants called "subshrubs" bridge the gap between perennials and shrubs. Although they are similar to perennials, subshrubs do in time grow a woody cell structure. Tree peonies, lavender, and rosemary are examples of subshrubs that are frequently classified as perennials and grown in perennial gardens.

True perennials are often referred to as "herbaceous perennials," with stems that are soft and fleshy rather than woody. In this book, we will deal mostly with herbaceous perennials. Some are evergreen, maintaining green leaves throughout winter, but most have top growth that dies down to the ground, surviving winter weather by means of vigorous roots that are better adapted for longevity than those of annuals or biennials. There is a large group of true perennials that can be grown as annuals to flower the first year, providing the seed is sown early enough. Some varieties of rudbeckias, such as gloriosa daisies, are examples of perennials that will flower the first year. The same is true with some varieties of delphinium, dianthus, and hollyhock *(Alcea rosea)*. The best example of a native perennial that plant breeders have developed to bloom the first year is the hardy hibiscus, 'Southern Belle.' Developed from *Hibiscus moscheutos,* native to southern swamps, Southern Belle grows flowers up to ten inches across in white, pink, or red, providing the seed is started early indoors and four-inch transplants can be set into the garden after the last frost date in spring. Though the seedlings are tender to frost, once established the plant will survive severe winter weather by means of its hardy root system, producing fresh green growth and an abundance of new flowers year after year.

Perennials are most often considered for beds and borders where an informal, natural look is desired in the landscape. Perennials can be mixed to obtain a succession of color from spring through autumn, or one kind can be planted in a mass to make a dramatic impact over a shorter period of time. Though most perennials are valued for their colorful flowers, a vast number are prized for their ornamental leaves. Foliage color in perennials is especially treasured because it generally lasts much longer than the fleeting beauty of other flowers. Ornamental grasses and ferns are good examples of this group. The color of the leaves is not the only facet to consider when planting mixed perennial beds and borders; texture and form are also important. The heavily veined leaves of some hostas, for example, are extremely attractive, while the wispy, graceful leaves of fountain grass are a beautiful highlight among perennials with broader leaves, such as hostas and lamb's ears *(Stachys byzantina).*

© Elizabeth Murray

Opposite page, left: In autumn, Claude Monet's garden at Giverney, France, features this border of perennial yellow sunflowers and purple Michaelmas daisies, plus annual nasturtiums and tuberous red dahlias.

Opposite page, right: Mixed beds of summer-flowering perennials interplanted with salad greens.

Right: Drifts of perennial sedum cover a sunny slope at Ohme Gardens, Wenatchee, Washington State.

CHAPTER ONE

DESIGNING WITH PERENNIALS

THERE ARE TWO WAYS TO PLANT PERENNIALS for color impact. One is to concentrate color for a particular season, such as early summer when most perennials reach peak bloom. Another is to spread color over an extended period so that something new is always coming into bloom. The latter is the most difficult to achieve—except in large gardens—without the help of annuals and flowering bulbs to fill in during the early and later months of the growing season.

Perennials are versatile plants for decorating a landscape, far more adaptable to a large range of soil types and light conditions than annuals or flowering bulbs. Only among perennials, for example, will you find flowering plants suitable for boggy soils and water gardens. Also, there is a far greater choice of flowering perennials suitable for shade.

To help you in your selections, see the chart on page 137 which gives approximate blooming times for the 100 choice perennial plants featured in this book.

Beds and Borders are the traditional way to effectively display perennials. Beds are usually planted in circular, oval, square, rectangular, or kidney shapes. Sometimes, they are triangular or pie-shaped when part of a cartwheel design. They are basically islands of soil, usually surrounded by lawn or paving material, with the soil mounded in the center to facilitate drainage and to provide a better display contour than a simple flat surface would. Borders have a backdrop—usually a wall, fence, or hedge with the soil elevated, sloping up to the rear.

One of the most impressive ways to use perennials in a garden is in a "double border," where parallel borders are divided by a path, ending in a focal point such as a gazebo, fountain, or bench. The effect is particularly attractive if the dividing strip is grass: but, where foot traffic is heavy, a paving material—such as brick or flagstone—can be used.

Since perennials come in a vast range of heights, varying from ground-hugging plants to tall plants, care must be taken so that the shorter ones are not screened by the taller ones. In island beds, concentrate tall plants in the middle and shorter ones around the edge. In a border, the tall plants should be placed in the rear and the short ones in the front.

Perennials generally have vigorous root systems, and therefore the soil for beds and borders should be dug deeply (to at least two feet) and enriched with plenty of organic material, such as well decomposed animal manure, leaf mold, garden compost, or peat (for more on how to prepare soil for planting perennials, see page 31).

Both beds and borders can be easily cared for by installing drip irrigation systems to provide moisture during dry spells, and by applying a weed-suffocating mulch to hide and protect the drip lines.

Rock Gardens are popular places to grow perennials, especially when there is a good balance between the color of the perennial plants and other design elements such as evergreen shrubs, rocks, and water. Perennials that creep and cascade over rough terrain are especially good to plant in rock gardens, particularly those that are drought tolerant,

Right: This intensively planted perennial garden features pink 'Autumn Joy' sedum, yellow rudbeckia, mauve astilbe, and blue hosta on both sides of a small stream.

Opposite page: This ornamental grass garden was designed by the landscape architects Oehme, van Sweden and Associates.

such as mountain phlox *(Phlox subulata)*, sedum, and echevaria. However, an easy-care form of rock garden is a dry wall, where large perennials can be planted along the top and smaller ones inserted between stones down the side. Low, spreading perennials—such as yellow alyssum and rock cress—are especially good for rock gardens and dry walls since they have the ability to drape over ledges and boulders.

Water Gardens take the form of an informal pond or a formal pool, where plants can be positioned on dry ground around the water to provide the drainage they need. There is also a large group of perennials called "bog plants" that thrive in permanently wet soil. In designing water gardens you should divide your plants into two distinct groups: those that like wet roots and those that are better suited to higher ground around the margin.

In formal pools, perennial plants are generally used sparingly if the architectural lines of the pool must complement other design elements, such as a nearby building. In this case, perennials are usually grown in containers sunk into the pool at strategic places so there is enough clear water between the plants to produce reflections.

In informal pools it is much more effective if the edges blur, with perennial plants spilling over into the water, billowing foliage contrasting with spiky foliage, creating a type of organized chaos.

Cutting Garden Many perennials with long stems are valued for the beautiful indoor floral arrangements that can be created with them. Though cutting flowers can be taken from display beds and borders, the overall color impact of the border will be reduced. Thus, many people prefer to have a special area set apart from the display area specifically for cutting, with flowers planted in regimented rows to make picking easy. Often, this area is adjacent to a vegetable garden since vegetables for the kitchen and perennials for arrangements can be conveniently picked at the same time.

Cut perennials will last a long time simply by immersing them in water soon after cutting. Lilies *(Lilium)*, gay feather *(Liatris spicata)*, asters, and shasta daisies *(Chrysanthemum x superbum)* are especially valued for cutting. Others—such as sea holly *(Eryngium maritimum)* and globe thistle *(Echinops ritro)*—are suitable for drying to create longer-lasting dried flower arrangements. A small group quickly wilt after cutting.

This can be stopped by sealing the cut end either by steeping it in boiling water for a few seconds or by scorching the ends. Poppies and dahlias are notable examples.

Don't just cut perennials for their flowers. Many have interesting foliage shapes, textures, and colors that can make floral arrangements more dramatic.

Shade Garden There are many different kinds of shade, from light shade where many different plants can grow, to deep shade where the choice of plant types is much more limited. The time of day that shade falls on a garden is also important. Some plants will flower poorly if shaded at noon, but will perform reasonably well when shaded during the morning or late afternoon. Likewise, many perennial wildflowers will bloom spectacularly in spring before the leaves are in full leaf, but woodland shade may be too heavy during mid-summer for many perennial varieties.

When shade is too great, measures can be taken to adjust the perennials to the environment. Even the removal of a single overhanging tree limb can make a noticeable difference. In fact, tests in light laboratories have shown that even 1 percent more light can mean a 100 percent improvement in plant performance.

Opposite page, left: a large mixed flower arrangement of garden perennials.
Opposite page, right: A small, simple, fresh flower arrangement of mixed varieties of chrysanthemums.
Left: A double perennial border at Glencoe Farm, Pennsylvania, reaches peak bloom in early summer.

The addition of brightly colored walls can help increase the amount of reflected light into a problem shade area; also, laying down a highly reflective mulch, such as white pebbles or landscape chips, can produce spectacular results.

In a heavily wooded area, don't be afraid to thin out the overhead tree canopy by selectively removing mature trees if too much shade is preventing the growth of your plants. If you cannot bring yourself to do this and would rather keep the area densely shaded, then consider an understory (a growth of plants low to the ground) of mostly foliage plants, such as ferns and hostas. The diversity of shapes, colors, and textures that can be obtained from just these two large perennial plant families is remarkable.

Opposite page: This beautiful perennial border was designed by artist Karen Kees at her home near San Diego, California. It was photographed in late March.
Left: Perennial white physostegia, yellow rudbeckia, and annual red salvia create a colorful flower bed in late summer.
Right: A dry wall richly planted with sun-loving perennials, including blue campanula, yellow and red rock rose, and purple fleabane.

Meadow Gardens Grasses and weeds are tenacious competition for a meadow garden. Many grasses are too aggressive and will crowd out cultivated perennials. However, some perennials can persist against grass competition. In a meadow garden it is possible to create spaces where clumps of perennials can be kept free of the encroaching grass. Some very good persistent perennials include species of tick-seed *(Coroepsis)*, cone flower *(Echinacea)*, daylilies *(Hemerocallis)*, loosestrife *(Lythrum)*, gay feather *(Liatris)*, and black-eyed Susan *(Rudbeckia)*. It's also possible to highlight a meadow garden by introducing some clump-forming ornamental grasses into it.

Don't expect to create a meadow garden by broadcasting perennial seeds like chicken feed among tall grasses and expect a harmonious field of wildflowers. Usually, it is far more successful if the entire area is plowed first. Then scatter a mixture containing both annual and perennial wildflower species onto bare soil. The annuals will bloom the first season and complete their life cycle, while the perennials will establish themselves during their first season and bloom strongly the next and subsequent years. Eventually, stubborn grasses and noxious weeds may begin to dominate and deplete the perennial flowering display, at which time the area can be plowed up and the process repeated.

Perennial Grass Garden Ornamental grass gardens have become extremely popular in recent years, particularly in places that are exposed to climatic extremes such as high winds and arid soil. At first, a border or garden of ornamental grasses may seem rather a boring prospect, but it is amazing how colorful a grass garden can be if the right varieties are chosen. For example, Japanese blood grass *(Imperata cylindrica rubra)* turns a brilliant crimson red color in autumn that is especially attractive when backlit by a rising or setting sun. Blue fescue *(Festuca glauca)* is a wonderful powder blue color that is accentuated even more dramatically on rainy days. Plus, there are many yellow and silver variegated forms of grasses.

In addition to the leaf colors, it's important to consider the flowering display some ornamental grasses produce. Most striking are the fluffy white plumes of pampas plume *(Cortadera selloana)* and the arching pink plumes of fountain grass *(Pennisetum setaceum)*.

Opposite page: This coastal garden on Long Island, New York, features a rich assortment of ornamental grasses, plus clump-forming perennials with colorful foliage.

Left: This rock garden successfully blends dwarf conifers with colorful perennials, including pink stonecrop sedum, red dragon's blood sedum, silvery lamb's ears, and yellow rudbeckia.

It's also possible to create striking contours with ornamental grasses by placing them in the landscape like cushions on a sofa. Many have billowing, cascading silhouettes with long, slender, arching leaves. Others have leaves that stand stiff and upright, while yet another group will lie prostrate to make a dense ground cover. Ornamental grasses can be planted to create hedges and screens, particularly for swimming pools and patios where the slightest rustle of leaves in the breeze can create the illusion of living in a serene and peaceful wilderness.

Most ornamental grass gardens undergo dramatic transformations in autumn, as their dried seed heads, shimmering in the sunlight, change color to wonderful shades of beige, russet, brown, and silver.

Perennial Fern Garden Consider fern gardens for shady places, especially under trees that cast high shade and beside water features such as streams, ponds, and pools. Though ferns are widely distributed throughout the world, surviving in both desert and arctic environments, the widest selection is best grown in a cool, moist environment. Even if you live in a region with severe winters where tropical ferns cannot survive outdoors, you can plant a tropical fern garden in tubs so they can be moved indoors during the winter. Two particularly good tree ferns are the Australian tree fern *(Alsophila australis)* and the Hawaiian tree fern *(Cybotium splendens),* both of which grow a healthy crown of fronds atop slender, dark brown trunks. Unfortunately, there are no hardy tree ferns. But, frost-exclusion is all that's necessary to keep the Australian tree fern healthy throughout the winter.

Ferns are best planted in groups, with each variety allowed a special territory within which to spread. Paths mulched with pine needles can wind through the clumps of ferns.

A water feature is particularly suited for a fern garden, especially a waterfall with ferns planted in pockets of soil among boulders, so that the droplets of splashing water soak the fern fronds.

Cushions of moss and clumps of hostas among ferns create a soothing, cooling environment.

Opposite page: This late-summer perennial border features orange helenium, yellow rudbeckia, and blue-mist shrubs.

Right: A small backyard perennial garden combines an appealing assortment of flower colors and leaf textures. Plants include purple liatris, yellow daylilies, striped ribbon grass, white shasta daisies, and lavender.

CHAPTER TWO

GROWING PERENNIALS

THERE ARE MANY WAYS THAT PERENNIALS can regenerate themselves. The least expensive and most popular method is generally by seed; this method of propagation allows hundreds—or even thousands—of plants to be reproduced for a fraction of a penny apiece. Sometimes a good method is to sow the seed in a specially prepared seed bed. When the seedlings are large enough to transplant they can be moved to permanent quarters in the garden. In this manner, you don't have to bother with starter pots or potting soil. However, it is advisable to locate the special seedling bed in a lightly shaded location to protect the young seedlings from sunburn. An alternate source of irrigation is also needed so that in case of insufficient rainfall, the seedlings can still be watered. Perennials can be sown into the soil from about mid-spring to mid-summer, allowing the majority of them to grow to a sturdy size by the time fall frosts occur and winter weather makes them dormant. Transplanted to their flowering positions in fall, perennials will remain dormant through the winter and then burst into glorious bloom in spring and summer.

Another seed-starting method is to grow perennials in starter pots during spring or summer, and transplant them to the garden in late summer, early fall, or the following spring if you can provide some protection, such as a cold frame, during severe winter weather. A cold frame is a miniature greenhouse—made of wood or aluminum—partially sunk into the soil, with a glass or plastic cover that can be vented during sunny days.

To grow perennials in starter pots, it's first necessary to germinate the seeds in a seed flat or a seed tray. Different perennials have different optimum temperature needs (and other idiosyncrasies), which normally will be printed on the seed packet. Once the seeds have germinated and are large enough to handle, they should be removed from the seed flat and individually potted. Two kinds of starter pots are popular—those made of plastic with a flexible bottom so that the soil and root ball can be popped up easily when you transplant, and those made of compressed peat. Roots will grow through the peat and, providing the bottom is torn loose to release the lower roots, the entire pot can be planted with minimum root disturbance and transplant shock.

BUYING PERENNIAL PLANTS

Many people do not have the time or the inclination to fuss with seeds, and would much rather buy started plants from a garden center or specialist mail-order nursery. In this case, there are distinct differences between the two sources of supply. Generally speaking, if you buy perennial plants from a local garden center your choice will be limited solely to the most popular types and varieties offered. To have access to more sophisticated varieties, and a much larger offering of hard-to-find species, you will have to turn to the list of sources on page 143 .

Perennials offered by mail are usually quite different from perennials you purchase in pots at a garden center. Mail-order perennials are generally supplied "bare-root"—wrapped in moist paper to keep the root from drying out. Or, the perennial will be growing in a small "plug"—a cone of soil with the roots forming a mesh that holds the soil together. These should be transplanted into the garden as soon as possible and watered regularly until they are well established. At the time of planting, you may need to gently open the root mass and pack soil in and around it to give the roots breathing space. Although spring is an ideal time to plant perennials, so, too, is fall since the cool conditions and the abundant moisture that prevail at that time of year generally allow the roots to grow strong before extremely cold weather makes them dormant.

ROOT DIVISIONS

A large group of perennials—such as daylilies *(Hemerocallis)*, bearded iris *(Iris germanica)*, and peonies *(Paeonia)*—take a long time to produce flowering-sized plants from seed, and in many cases the resulting progeny may be a mixture of different colors. If you do not want to wait, root division is a quicker way to increase your stock of this particular group of perennials. After several years, most perennials will form thick clumps of roots or bulbs that are easily divided in the spring or fall. Depending on the size of the mother clump, you will normally need a garden fork to dig up the root mass and separate it into smaller clumps. Usually, the clump will show growing tips where new foliage will appear. Providing each division has a minimum of three growing points, the clump is likely to make good progress when transplanted.

Some perennials have such vigorous root systems that all it takes to grow a new plant is a small piece of root, called a root cutting. But, it can be tedious cutting roots so small, and simple division will ensure a higher rate of success.

Above: Bearded iris rhizomes prior to dividing.
Below: The same bearded iris rhizomes after dividing and ready for transplanting.

1. Thick perennial clumps may need separating into smaller clumps by using garden forks to make divisions.

2. Separate smaller clumps by hand, ensuring each clump has a healthy growing crown and roots.

3. Lift clump with fork or spade. Wash away large clumps of soil. Pull and separate into divisions, each division containing new growth or buds, old stems, and a root system.

4. In the ground, a typical perennial clump will look like this—with the thick root ball hollow in the middle. Sometimes new growth is not as obvious as shown here, especially in fall after frost.

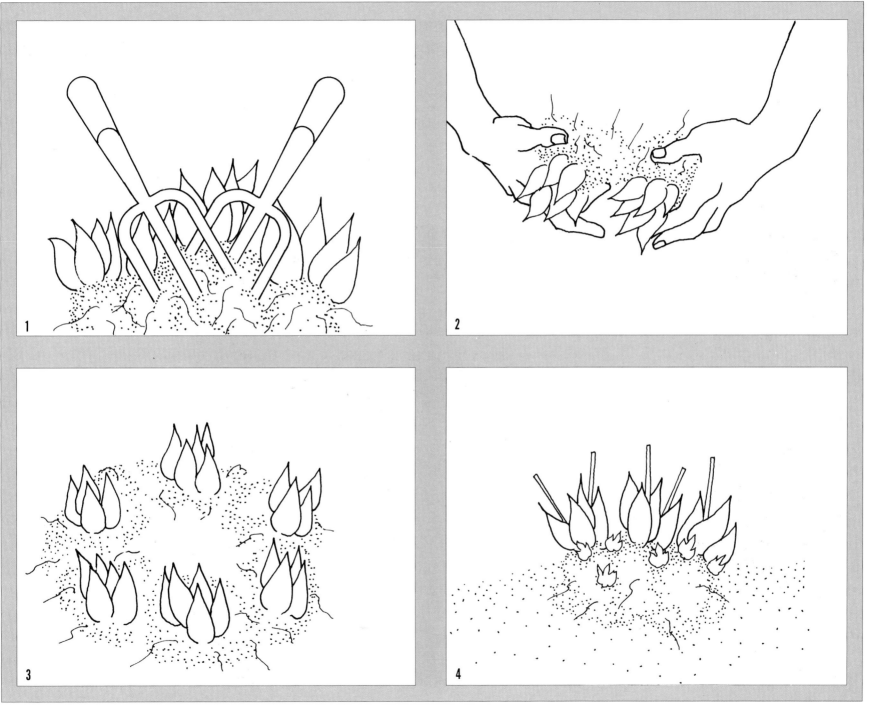

STEM CUTTINGS

A vast number of perennials readily root themselves from stem sections, called stem cuttings. Carnations (*Dianthus caryophyllus*), asters, and chrysanthemums are popular perennials frequently increased by stem cuttings. Usually, a four- to six-inch section of new growth on side shoots is cut on a slant just below the leaf joint. Leaves in the lower half are removed so that just a crown of leaves at the top of the cutting remains. The bare stem section is treated with a rooting hormone (available from garden centers) and inserted into a moist potting soil, such as a peat-perlite mixture. Normally, a seed flat is used so that dozens of cuttings can be rooted at one time. Place the flat under light shade in a cold frame or under a plastic cover for protection until the cuttings are well rooted. Keep the soil moist. After a period of about four to six weeks you should be able to tug on one of the cuttings to find if it has developed a healthy root system along the bare section of stem.

On a smaller scale, cuttings can be rooted in eight- or ten-inch clay pots placed on a bright windowsill indoors. Avoid direct sunlight since cuttings are easily burned, especially under glass, and do not allow the soil to dry out.

Left: This dramatic perennial border features perennial white shasta daisies, plumes of white salvia, blue globe bellflower, and orange-flowered annual cosmos.

1. Cut off a 5-inch-long side shoot.

2. Remove lower leaves.

3. Dip end in rooting hormone.

4. Set firmly in soil mix.

5. and 6. Place cuttings in propagator, made from seed flat, with plastic cover.

7. Alternatively, use deep box covered with glass.

8. Set out in cold frames during winter.

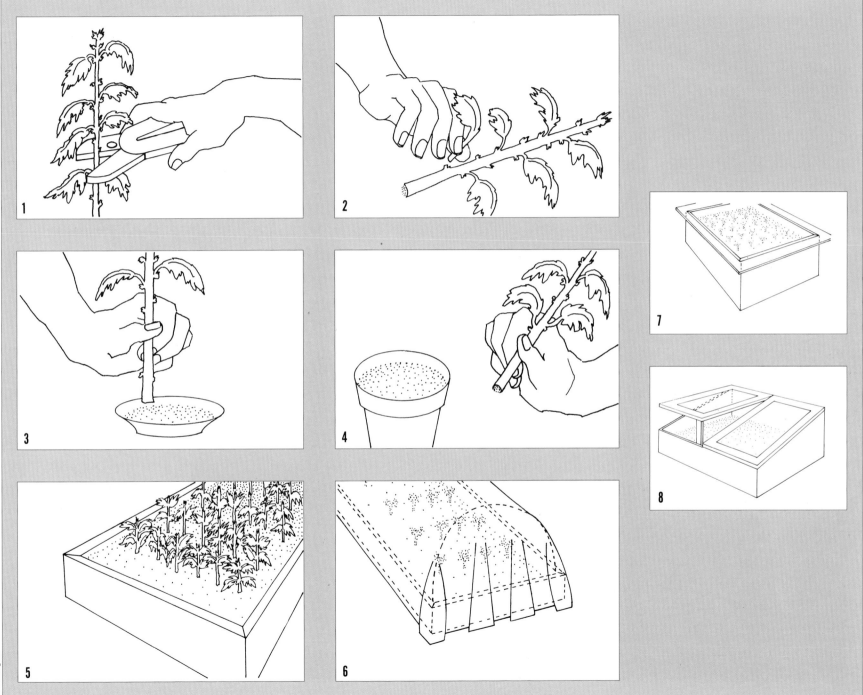

A. M. Georgens

Left: Perennial phlox light up this perennial border in early summer.

Opposite page, left: Here, perennial lavender is protected in the winter by a mulch of pine needles applied after the first frost.

Opposite page, above: Viola plants set out into their flowering positions in autumn are protected with a mulch of attractive pine needles so they will bloom early in spring.

Opposite page, below: Here, perennial plants have been mulched with decorative pine bark to deter weeds and conserve soil moisture.

SOIL PREPARATION

Perennials are mostly planted in beds and borders. Although many are tolerant of poor soil and dry conditions, generally they are heavy feeders, requiring not only a fertile soil high in organic matter, but also one that is crumbly to a depth of at least two feet, with good moisture retention and good drainage of excess moisture. Soil that is excessively sandy or contains a lot of clay is not good for perennials. In both cases the addition of large amounts of well decomposed animal manure, compost, leaf mold, or peat moss may be necessary to bring the soil up to standard.

In soil with high acidity (generally found in areas with high rainfall) the addition of lime may be necessary every three years at the rate of 5 pounds per 100 square feet. In soil that contains high alkaline it may be necessary to build a raised bed of stones or landscape ties above the indigenous soil, and truck in a soil with low alkalinity or neutral pH.

A good way to get the necessary soil depth for beds and borders is to raise the planting area. Mound the soil so it stands about twelve inches above the original soil level, and edge the bed with stone or landscape ties to keep it in place.

To conserve soil moisture it is a good practice to incorporate some kind of "mulch"—a covering over the soil that deters weeds and retains moisture—into it. Good mulch materials for perennials include shredded bark, wood chips, straw, shredded leaves, leaf mold, and garden compost. A soil that is topped each year with compost will generally keep perennials in good health. Where compost is not available to do this, a general-purpose granular fertilizer—such as 10–10–10—should be scattered over the soil in early spring and carefully raked into the upper inch of the soil. The numbers 10–10–10 refer to the percentages of major plant nutrients in a fertilizer formula. In this case: 10 percent nitrogen, 10 percent phosphorus, and 10 percent potash. The remaining 70 percent of this fertilizer is "filler" that acts as a distributing agent.

CHAPTER THREE

THE ENCYCLOPEDIA OF ESSENTIAL PERENNIALS

THE FOLLOWING 100 SUPERLATIVE PERENNI-ALS for garden display have been chosen for their ornamental value, many with gorgeous flowering displays, others for their decorative leaves.

They are listed alphabetically by their botanical (Latin) name because this most consistently identifies garden perennials better than their common names. While many have popular common names—'Johnny Jump-up' for *Viola tricolor*—others are not as common or are known by two or more common names— *Yucca filamentosa,* for example, is often called 'Yucca,' 'Desert Candle,' or 'Adam's Needle.'

To find a description for any perennial where you know only the common name, simply refer to the index for a quick cross-reference.

The heights given are mostly mature heights, when the plants start to flower. Often, with good soil or abundant rainfall, or late in the season, plants may exceed the heights stated here.

BOTANICAL NAME *Acanthus mollis*

COMMON NAME Bear's-breech

RANGE Native to Mediterranean. Hardy zone 8 south.

HEIGHT 4 feet; spreading habit.

CULTURE Tender. Needs cool, moist soil in sun or shade. Propagated by root division. Blooms in early summer.

DESCRIPTION Large, deeply indented, glossy green leaves are highly ornamental, creating a tropical, shrublike appearance. Flowers are pale purple, borne on long, slender flower spikes. Popular in coastal locations. Good garden accent used singly; also useful as a ground cover for large expanses of moist soil. Flower spikes make good dried arrangements.

BOTANICAL NAME *Achillea filipendulina*

COMMON NAME Yellow Yarrow

RANGE Native to Europe and Asia. Hardy zone 4 south.

HEIGHT 3 to 4 feet; upright, spreading habit.

CULTURE Easy to grow in any well-drained garden soil in full sun. Propagated by root division. Blooms in spring.

DESCRIPTION An invasive plant forming dense clumps of fern-like, aromatic leaves. Flat flower panicles are borne on slender stems in shades of yellow, mostly golden yellow and pale yellow. A related species, *A. millefolium* has rosy red flowers. Effective in mixed beds and borders. Good for cutting and adding fragrance to potpourris.

RECOMMENDED VARIETY 'Moonshine.'

BOTANICAL NAME *Aegopodium podagraria* "variegatum"

COMMON NAME Bishop's-weed

RANGE Native to Europe and Asia. Hardy zone 4 south.

HEIGHT 12 inches; low, spreading habit.

CULTURE Easy to grow in any well-drained garden soil in full sun. Propagated by root division in spring or fall. Blooms early summer, but grown more for its attractive leaves.

DESCRIPTION Ivy-shaped leaves form a dense mat, making this an ideal ground cover, especially for edging paths. Light green leaves have a white margin. Flowers are white like Queen Anne's Lace, borne on long, slender stems. Flower stems can be used as a cut flower.

BOTANICAL NAME *Ajuga reptans*

COMMON NAME Blue Bugle

RANGE Native to Europe. Hardy zone 3 south.

HEIGHT 3 to 6 inches; low, rosette-forming habit.

CULTURE Easy to grow in any well-drained garden soil. Propagated by division of offsets in spring or fall. Spring-blooming.

DESCRIPTION Plants form attractive ground-hugging rosettes of evergreen, dark green, crinkled leaves. Bronze leaf and variegated forms are also available. Attractive blue or white flower spikes appear in spring. Best used as a ground cover for edging paths and as drifts in rock gardens.

RECOMMENDED VARIETY 'Burgundy Glow' with white and pink variegated foliage.

BOTANICAL NAME *Alcea rosea*

COMMON NAME Hollyhocks

RANGE Native to China. Hardy zone 4 south.

HEIGHT 6 feet; upright habit.

CULTURE Prefers moist, fertile loam soil in full sun. Propagated mostly by seed. Summer-flowering.

DESCRIPTION Tall flower spikes are studded with cup-size satinlike flowers in red, pink, yellow, and white. Both single and double flower forms are popular. Leaves are large, green, ivy-shaped. Good to use for tall backgrounds in mixed borders. Also popular to grow against walls, along fence rows, and beside garden structures such as tool sheds.

BOTANICAL NAME *Alchemilla mollis*

COMMON NAME Lady's-mantle

RANGE Native to Europe. Hardy zone 4 south.

HEIGHT 1 to 2 feet; prostrate, spreading habit.

CULTURE Prefers moist, humus-rich soil in sun or partial shade. Propagated by root division. Spring-blooming.

DESCRIPTION Yellow flowers are borne in dense clusters and are highly ornamental, though plants are also grown for their silvery leaves that form bushy clumps. Popular for edging garden pools and as an accent in mixed beds and borders.

A double perennial border featuring, in the foreground, an effective companion planting of daylilies and artemisia 'Silver Queen.'

A walled perennial garden at Old Westbury Gardens, Long Island, features mostly purple foxglove and bearded iris.

BOTANICAL NAME *Amsonia tabernaemontana*

COMMON NAME Blue-star

RANGE Native to North America. Hardy zone 4 south.

HEIGHT 2 feet; bushy habit.

CULTURE Prefers moist, well-drained loam soil in full sun. Propagated by root division. Spring-flowering.

DESCRIPTION Masses of pale blue flowers are borne in clusters on long stems. The willow-like leaves give the plants a graceful appearance. Good accent for mixed beds and borders. Suitable for cutting.

BOTANICAL NAME *Anchusa azurea*

COMMON NAME Italian Bugloss

RANGE Native to Europe. Hardy zone 4 south.

HEIGHT 3 to 5 feet; erect habit.

CULTURE Prefers moist, well-drained loam soil in full sun. Propagated mostly by seed and root division. May need staking. Early summer-flowering.

DESCRIPTION Flowers resemble a large Forget-me-not, azure blue, clustered at the top of slender stems. Leaves are long, pointed. Popular as an accent in mixed beds and borders. Good for cutting. The variety 'Little John' is a dwarf, compact type producing a 12-inch high mound suitable for mass planting.

BOTANICAL NAME *Anemone* x *hybrida*

COMMON NAME Japanese Anemone

RANGE Hybrids of species native to Japan. Hardy zone 5 south.

HEIGHT Up to 5 feet; upright, clump-forming habit.

CULTURE Prefers moist, humus-rich loam soil in sun or partial shade. Propagated by root division in spring. May need staking. Late summer-flowering.

DESCRIPTION Masses of lovely white and pink flowers resembling single and semi-double roses are held erect on slender stems. Leaves are dark green, sharply indented. Popular accent in mixed beds and borders. Good for cutting.

RECOMMENDED VARIETIES 'Whirlwind,' a semi-double white. These plants are sometimes sold as *A. japonica*.

BOTANICAL NAME *Anemone pulsatilla*

COMMON NAME Pasqueflower

RANGE Native to Europe and Asia. Hardy zone 5 south.

HEIGHT 12 inches; low, mound-shaped habit.

CULTURE Prefers well-drained alkaline or neutral soil in full sun. Propagated by seed and division in early spring. Early spring-flowering.

DESCRIPTION Lovely bell-shaped purple flowers are borne on arching stems above a clump of silvery, finely dissected leaves. Hybrid forms are available in white, rose red, and pink. Wonderful accent for rock gardens, especially planted in drifts among creeping phlox to create a miniature alpine meadow.

BOTANICAL NAME *Anthemis tinctoria*

COMMON NAME Golden Marguerite

RANGE Native to Europe. Hardy zone 4 south.

HEIGHT 3 feet; bushy habit.

CULTURE Tolerates a wide range of soils with good drainage in sun or partial shade. Propagated by seed and root division. Summer-flowering.

DESCRIPTION Yellow, daisy-like flowers are formed in abundance on long stems. Leaves are finely toothed, fragrant, fern-like. Popular for mixed beds and borders. Good for cutting.

RECOMMENDED VARIETY 'Kelwayi,' a golden yellow.

RELATED SPECIES *A. nobilis* ('Chamomile'), forming dark green cushions with yellow, buttonlike flowers.

BOTANICAL NAME *Aquilegia* hybrids

COMMON NAME Columbine

RANGE Developed from species native to North America. Hardy zone 5 south.

HEIGHT 2 to 3 feet; upright, airy habit.

CULTURE Prefers fertile loam soil in sun or partial shade. Propagated mostly by seed. Spring-flowering.

DESCRIPTION Unusual nodding flowers are shaped like granny's bonnets, with elegant, long spurs, held high above the foliage on slender stems. Leaves are gray green, deeply indented. Popular for mixed beds and borders. Exquisite cut flower.

RECOMMENDED VARIETY "McKana Giants,' which will bloom the first year if sown in January or February.

RELATED SPECIES *A. caerulea* (a gorgeous blue and white bicolor) and *A. canadensis* (a red and yellow bicolor).

BOTANICAL NAME *Arabis caucasica*

COMMON NAME Rock-cress, Wall-cress

RANGE Native to Europe. Hardy zone 4 south.

HEIGHT 12 inches; low, ground-hugging habit.

CULTURE Easy to grow in any well-drained garden soil in sun or partial shade. Propagated by seed and root division. Early spring-flowering.

DESCRIPTION Dainty, white, four-petaled flowers cover the spreading plants. Dark green leaves are spear-shaped. Popular for rock gardens and dry walls, also edging paths, beds, and borders.

BOTANICAL NAME *Armeria maritima*

COMMON NAME Common Thrift

RANGE Native to coastlines of Europe. Hardy zone 4 south.

HEIGHT 12 inches; mounded, ground-hugging habit.

CULTURE Prefers well-drained, sandy soil. Salt tolerant. Propagated by seed and division. Spring-flowering.

DESCRIPTION Globular pink or white flower clusters grow atop slender stems above a cushion of gray-green evergreen needlelike leaves. Excellent for seaside gardens. Creates a good ground cover planted in a mass. Useful to edge beds and borders. Popular in rock gardens and dry walls.

BOTANICAL NAME *Artemesia ludoviciana*

COMMON NAME Silver King

RANGE Native to North America. Hardy zone 5 south.

HEIGHT 3 feet; erect, bushy habit.

CULTURE Easy to grow in any well-drained soil in full sun. Propagated mostly by root division. Grown mostly for its foliage color.

DESCRIPTION Silver King artemesia has inconspicuous white flowers and is grown mainly for its silvery foliage that remains colorful all summer and into autumn. Plants are especially effective when mixed with pink flowers to give an old-fashioned look to perennial beds and borders. The leaves are narrow, toothed. Popular for cutting both fresh and dried.

RELATED SPECIES *A. schmidtiana*, resembling a silver cushion.

BOTANICAL NAME *Arum italicum*

COMMON NAME Italian Arum

RANGE Native to the Mediterranean. Hardy zone 6 south.

HEIGHT 12 inches; low, mounded habit.

CULTURE Prefers moist, acidic, humus-rich soil in partial shade. Propagated by seed and by division of dormant tubers. Grown mostly for its leaf shape and late summer berry display.

DESCRIPTION Attractive arrow-shaped leaves appear in spring, immediately following the appearance of a greenish white flower spathe resembling a small Calla Lily or Jack-in-the-pulpit. However, its principal ornamental value is the cluster of bright red berries that ripens on top of each flower stalk in late summer and persists into early autumn. Good to grow in woodland gardens along stream banks or pond margins.

RECOMMENDED VARIETY 'Pictum' with green and white variegated leaves.

This perennial garden at Van Dusen Botanical Gardens, Vancouver, British Columbia, blends yellow and pink flowers in a striking color combination. Plants include yellow verbascum, rose campion, and pink fleabane.

BOTANICAL NAME *Asclepias tuberosa*

COMMON NAME Butterfly Milkweed

RANGE Native to North America. Hardy zone 4 south.

HEIGHT 2 to 3 feet; upright, clump-forming habit.

CULTURE Prefers well-drained loam or sandy soil in full sun. Propagated by seed or root division. Drought resistant. Summer-flowering.

DESCRIPTION Brilliant clusters of orange flowers freely produced on bushy plants. Slender stems have narrow, pointed green leaves. Popular for growing in meadows where it competes favorably with grasses. Also good to grow in mixed beds and borders. Excellent for cutting.

RECOMMENDED VARIETY 'Gay Butterflies,' a mixture that includes yellow, red, and pink.

BOTANICAL NAME *Aster novae-angliae*

COMMON NAME Michaelmas Daisy

RANGE Native to New England. Hardy zone 4 south.

HEIGHT 3 to 5 feet; erect, billowing habit.

CULTURE Prefers moist, fertile, well-drained loam soil. Propagated by root division. May need stalking. Late summer-flowering.

DESCRIPTION Daisy-like pink, purple, and white flowers have golden yellow centers, are borne in profusion on bushy plants with finely toothed green leaves. Excellent for garden display in mixed beds and borders. Tall kinds especially good for backgrounds. Suitable for cutting.

RECOMMENDED VARIETY 'Alma Potschke' (deep pink).

RELATED SPECIES AND HYBRIDS *A.* x *frikartii* 'Wonder of Staffa' (lavender blue) and *A. tartaricus* (violet blue from Siberia).

BOTANICAL NAME *Astilbe* x *arendsii*

COMMON NAME False Spirea

RANGE Hybrids of species native to China. Hardy zone 5 south.

HEIGHT 2 to 4 feet; upright, clump-forming habit.

CULTURE Prefers moist, fertile, loam soil in partial shade. Propagated by root division. Early summer-flowering.

DESCRIPTION Spires of pink, red, and white flower clusters are borne in profusion above shrublike plants with sharply indented leaves. Popular for mixed beds and borders, and for the margins of ponds and steams. Excellent for cutting.

RECOMMENDED VARIETY 'Fanal' (dark red) and 'Ostrich Plume' (coral pink).

RELATED SPECIES *A. chinensis* 'Pumila' (dwarf, light pink) and *A. taquetii* ('Superba' tall, deep pink with extra-long flower plumes).

BOTANICAL NAME *Aubrieta deltoide*

COMMON NAME False Rock-cress

RANGE Native to Europe. Hardy zone 5 south.

HEIGHT 6 inches; low, spreading habit.

CULTURE Tolerates poor soils providing drainage is good in sun or partial shade. Propagated by seed and root division. Spring-flowering.

DESCRIPTION Dainty, four-petaled flowers cover the mound-shaped plants in pink or purple. Leaves are oval, pointed. Very popular in rock gardens and dry walls. Also good for edging paths, beds, and borders.

BOTANICAL NAME *Aurinia saxatilis*

COMMON NAME Basket of Gold; Perennial Alyssum

RANGE Native to Europe. Hardy zone 4 south.

HEIGHT 12 inches; mounded, clump-forming habit.

CULTURE Prefers well-drained sandy or gritty soil in full sun. Propagated by seed and stem cuttings. Flowers in early spring.

DESCRIPTION Tiny golden yellow flowers are formed in dense clusters on spreading plants with gray-green narrow, pointed leaves. Popular for dry walls and rock gardens; also good for edging beds and borders. The variety 'Citrina' has pale yellow flowers.

BOTANICAL NAME *Baptisia australis*

COMMON NAME Blue Wild Indigo

RANGE Native to North America. Hardy zone 4 south.

HEIGHT 3 to 4 feet; upright, bushy habit.

CULTURE Prefers a sandy loam soil with excellent drainage in full sun. Drought tolerant. Propagated by seed and root division. Spring-flowering.

DESCRIPTION Lupin-like blue flowers are formed on strong stems. Clover-like leaves are bright green. Useful as an accent in mixed beds and borders. Excellent for cutting.

BOTANICAL NAME *Bergenia cordifolia*

COMMON NAME Heartleaf Bergenia

RANGE Native to Siberia. Hardy zone 3 south.

HEIGHT 12 inches; rosette, ground-hugging habit.

CULTURE Prefers moist, humus-rich loam soil in partial shade. Propagated mostly by root division. Early spring-flowering.

DESCRIPTION Clusters of pink flowers are produced on long stems above a rosette of fleshy, cabbage-like evergreen leaves that are usually tinted red. Popular for creating a ground cover under trees and along stream banks or pond margins. Also used in rock gardens. Many good hybrids have been introduced, such as 'Silver Light' (white-flowered) and 'Sunningdale' with carmine flowers.

BOTANICAL NAME *Caltha palustris*

COMMON NAME Marsh-marigold

RANGE Native to Northern Europe. Hardy zone 4 south.

HEIGHT 12 inches; mounded, clump-forming habit.

CULTURE Prefers moist, fertile, humus-rich soil in partial shade. Tolerates boggy conditions. Propagated by seed and root division. Early spring-flowering.

DESCRIPTION Conspicuous buttercup-like flowers are shimmering golden yellow, in single or double forms. Leaves are glossy dark green, heart-shaped. Popular in woodland gardens where soil remains moist. Excellent accent for pond margins and stream banks.

RECOMMENDED VARIETY 'Flore Pleno' with large, double flowers.

This wild woodland garden sparkles with perennial species of white foam flower, yellow primrose, blue woodland phlox, and red columbine.

A simple border of chrysanthemums brightens this house foundation in autumn.

BOTANICAL NAME *Campanula glomerata*

COMMON NAME Globe Bellflower

RANGE Native to Europe. Hardy zone 4 south.

HEIGHT 2 to 3 feet; upright habit.

CULTURE Prefers moist, fertile loam soil in full sun. Propagated by seed or root division. Early summer-flowering.

DESCRIPTION Beautiful blue or white bell-shaped flowers are clustered into a globe shape on slender stems. Mint green leaves are narrow, pointed. Popular in mixed beds and borders. Excellent for cutting.

BOTANICAL NAME *Campanula percisifolia*

COMMON NAME Willow-leaf Bellflower

RANGE Native to Europe. Hardy zone 4 south.

HEIGHT 2 to 3 feet; erect, clump-forming habit.

CULTURE Easy to grow in any moist, well-drained garden soil in full sun. Propagated by seed and root division. Spring-flowering.

DESCRIPTION Large bell-shaped flowers in blue or white are crowded along slender stems. Leaves are narrow, willow-like. Popular in mixed beds and borders. Good for cutting.

RELATED SPECIES *C. latifolia* ('Great Bellflower').

BOTANICAL NAME *Catananche caerulea*

COMMON NAME Cupid's-dart

RANGE Native to the Mediterranean. Hardy zone 5 south.

HEIGHT 2 to 3 feet; upright clump-forming habit.

CULTURE Easy to grow in any well-drained garden soil in full sun. Drought-resistant. Propagated by seed or root division. Summer-flowering.

DESCRIPTION Pale blue cornflower-like blooms are held erect on slender stems. Leaves are gray-green, grasslike. Popular for mixed beds and borders. Excellent for cutting in both fresh and dried arrangements.

BOTANICAL NAME *Centranthus ruber*

COMMON NAME Red Valerian

RANGE Native to the Mediterranean. Hardy zone 5 south.

HEIGHT 2 to 3 feet; upright, bushy habit.

CULTURE Thrives in a wide range of well-drained soils in full sun. Propagated by seeds and root cuttings. Spring- and early summer-flowering.

DESCRIPTION Small red, pink, or white flowers form showy clusters on long, slender stems. Leaves are gray-green, narrow, pointed. Does best in cool coastal locations where it self-sows readily. Good for rock gardens and dry walls, also mixed beds and borders. Excellent cut flower.

BOTANICAL NAME *Cerastium tomentosum*

COMMON NAME Snow-in-summer

RANGE Native to Europe. Hardy zone 4 south.

HEIGHT 6 inches; ground hugging, spreading habit.

CULTURE Easy to grow in any well-drained soil in full sun. Propagated by seed and root division. Late spring-, early summer-flowering.

DESCRIPTION Small white flowers almost smother the foliage, creating a carpet of white, like drifts of snow. Gray, narrow leaves are covered with silvery hairs. Popular for rock gardens and dry walls. Also good for edging mixed beds and borders.

BOTANICAL NAME *Chrysanthemum* x *morifolium*

COMMON NAME Garden Mum; Cushion Mum

RANGE Hybrids of species mostly native to China. Hardy zone 5 south.

HEIGHT 1 to 2 feet; mounded habit.

CULTURE Prefers moist, fertile well-drained loam soil in full sun. Propagated by stem cuttings and root division. To maintain a good dome shape with lots of basal branches, growing tip should be pinched in spring and summer. Winter hardiness is highly variable depending on variety. Mostly autumn-flowering.

DESCRIPTION Flower shape and color among garden chrysanthemums is extremely varied, from pompom flowers and daisy flowers to "spiders" and "spoons," in yellow, red, orange, bronze, purple, and white. Leaves are dark green, narrow, and toothed. Popular for massing in beds, edging borders, and container planting. Tall types are good for cutting.

Daylilies are one of the best perennials for summer color in beds and borders.

BOTANICAL NAME *Chrysanthemum parthenium*

COMMON NAME Feverfew

RANGE Native to Mediterranean. Hardy zone 4 south.

HEIGHT 2 to 3 feet; erect, bushy habit.

CULTURE Easy to grow in any well-drained garden soil in full sun. Self-seeds readily and needs rigorous thinning to keep it in bounds. Propagated by seed and root division. Late spring- and summer-flowering.

DESCRIPTION Small, white, daisy-like flowers have conspicuous yellow centers. Double, buttonlike forms also available. Leaves are typical chrysanthemum shape, finely toothed. Popular in mixed beds and borders as a cloudlike accent. Excellent cut flower.

BOTANICAL NAME *Chrysanthemum* x *superbum*

COMMON NAME Shasta Daisy

RANGE Native to Europe. Hardy zone 5 south.

HEIGHT 1 to 3 feet; upright, bushy habit.

CULTURE Prefers moist, fertile, well-drained loam soil in full sun. Propagated by seed and root divisions. Young plants need the tip growth pinching to encourage bushy habit. Summer-flowering.

DESCRIPTION White, daisy-like flowers have golden yellow centers. Some varieties are double flowered. Individual flowers can measure up to 5 inches across. Sometimes confused with *C. leucanthemum* ('Ox-Eye Daisy') which is smaller flowered and blooms a month earlier than Shasta Daisy. Dark green leaves are slender, toothed. Popular for display in mixed beds and borders. Excellent for cutting. Dwarf varieties, such as 'Miss Muffet,' are suitable for containers and edging.

BOTANICAL NAME *Cimicifuga racemosa*

COMMON NAME Snakeroot

RANGE Native to North America. Hardy zone 3 south.

HEIGHT 6 feet; towering, erect, spirelike habit.

CULTURE Prefers moist, fertile, humus-rich soil in partial shade. Propagated by root division. May need staking. Summer-flowering.

DESCRIPTION Beautiful, tall, flower spikes are crowded with tiny white or creamy flowers. Leaves are dark green, fern-like, finely toothed. Popular for woodland gardens and as a background in mixed beds and borders.

RELATED SPECIES *C. simplex*, only 4 feet tall and flowers later.

BOTANICAL NAME *Coreopsis lanceolata*

COMMON NAME Lance-Leaf Coreopsis

RANGE Native to North America. Hardy zone 4 south.

HEIGHT 2 to 3 feet; upright habit.

CULTURE Easy to grow in any well-drained soil in full sun. Propagated by seed and root division. May need staking in fertile soils. Summer-flowering.

DESCRIPTION Bright yellow, daisy-like flowers are borne in profusion on long, slender stems. Leaves are narrow, spear-shaped. Popular for mixed beds and borders. Also wildflower meadows.

RECOMMENDED VARIETY 'Goldfink' (dwarf, compact). Good for cutting.

RELATED SPECIES *C. verticillata* ('Thread-leaf Coreopsis') growing mounds of airy foliage and yellow, star-shaped flowers.

BOTANICAL NAME *Delphinium elatum*

COMMON NAME English Delphinium

RANGE Native to Siberia. Hardy zone 4.

HEIGHT 6 feet; erect, spirelike habit.

CULTURE Prefers moist, fertile, loam soil in full sun. Propagated mostly by seeds. May need staking. Except in regions with cool summers like the Pacific Northwest, Delphinium are best grown as annuals or biennials, since harsh winters and hot summers tend to exhaust them. Summer-flowering.

DESCRIPTION Stout flowering stems are studded with single and double flowers that have contrasting white or black centers called "bees." Color range includes blue, purple, white, and pink. Popular as tall backgrounds for beds and borders. Sensational for cutting.

RECOMMENDED VARIETIES 'Pacific Hybrids' with extra large flower spikes and 'Blue Heaven' a dwarf, bushy variety.

BOTANICAL NAME *Dianthus plumarius*

COMMON NAME Cottage Pinks

RANGE Native to Europe. Hardy zone 4 south.

HEIGHT 12 inches; low, mounded, ground-hugging habit.

CULTURE Easy to grow in any well-drained soil in full sun. Propagated by seed and root division. Spring-flowering.

DESCRIPTION Fragrant, carnation-like double flowers, mostly with fringed petals. Colors include white, pink, rose red, and purple. Often bicolored. Leaves blue-gray, evergreen, grasslike. Popular for rock gardens and dry walls, also for edging mixed beds and borders. Superb cut flowers. Many beautiful hybrids have been created.

RELATED SPECIES *D. deltoides* ('Maiden Pinks'), *D. gratianopolitanus* ('Cheddar Pinks') and *D.* x *allwoodii* ('Allwood Pinks')—all of which are smaller-flowered and generally more dwarf and compact, making them suitable for rock gardens.

BOTANICAL NAME *Dicentra spectabilis*

COMMON NAME Japanese Bleeding-heart

RANGE Native to Japan. Hardy zone 2 south.

HEIGHT 2 to 3 feet; bushy habit.

CULTURE Prefers light, acidic, well-drained soil in sun or partial shade. Propagated by root division in spring. Spring-flowering.

DESCRIPTION Heart-shaped pink or white flowers are borne on graceful arching stems. The finely cut, gray-green leaves die down during hot weather but the roots remain viable and survive. Winters in dormant condition. Excellent display plant for shady mixed borders.

RELATED SPECIES *D. eximia* ('Eastern Bleeding Heart') and *D. formosa* ('Western Bleeding Heart') are native to the United States, more compact in habit, also popular for beds and borders.

BOTANICAL NAME *Digitalis purpurea*

COMMON NAME English Foxglove

RANGE Native to Europe. Hardy zone 4 south.

HEIGHT 5 feet; towering, erect habit.

CULTURE Prefers moist, fertile, humus-rich soil in partial shade. Propagated by seeds. Early summer-flowering.

DESCRIPTION Though truly a biennial, English Foxgloves appear to be perennial since they reseed themselves so easily and generally come back year after year. Purple, tubular flowers with handsome freckles in the throats are crowded along tall, slender, flower spikes. Leaves are thick, coarse, pointed. Excellent for backgrounds in mixed beds and borders. Also popular in woodland wildflower gardens. A hybrid variety, 'Excelsior,' has white, pink, and yellow flowers.

RELATED SPECIES *D. grandiflora* ('Yellow Foxglove') is a true perennial form propagated by division, producing lovely yellow flower spikes. All species are excellent for cutting.

A beautiful mass planting of delphinium enjoy cool conditions in the rose garden at Butchart Gardens, Victoria, British Columbia.

BOTANICAL NAME *Doronicum caucasicum*

COMMON NAME Dogbane

RANGE Native to China. Hardy zone 3 south.

HEIGHT 2 feet; upright, spreading habit.

CULTURE Prefers rich, moist, loam soil in full sun. Propagated by seed and by root division in early spring. Early spring-flowering.

DESCRIPTION Golden yellow, daisy-like flowers appear on long stems. Coarse, pointed, toothed leaves form dense, spreading mats that may need dividing after several years. Popular for mixed borders and rock gardens. Excellent for cutting.

BOTANICAL NAME *Echinacea purpurea*

COMMON NAME Purple Coneflower

RANGE Native to North America. Hardy zone 3 south.

HEIGHT 3 to 6 feet; upright habit.

CULTURE Tolerates poor soil; may need staking if soil is moist and fertile. Prefers full sun. Propagated by seed and by root division. Forms clumps that may need dividing after several years. Summer-flowering.

DESCRIPTION Flowers have a rakish profile pointing skyward. A large cone-shaped crown of brown anthers has purple petals that sweep back. Good for garden display, especially in mixed borders.

BOTANICAL NAME *Echinops ritro*

COMMON NAME Small Globe-thistle

RANGE Native to the Mediterranean. Hardy zone 3 south.

HEIGHT 3 to 5 feet; billowing habit.

CULTURE Prefers fertile loam soil in full sun. Generally needs staking. Propagated mostly by seed and root division. Summer-flowering.

DESCRIPTION Steel blue, globe-shaped flowers are borne in profusion on long stems. Popular for mixed borders. Beloved by flower arrangers for fresh flower arrangements and as dried flowers.

RECOMMENDED VARIETY 'Taplow Blue.'

BOTANICAL NAME *Erigeron* hybrids

COMMON NAME Fleabane

RANGE Native species grow from Southern California to the Pacific Northwest. Hardy zone 6 south.

HEIGHT 1 to 2 feet; bushy, spreading habit.

CULTURE Tolerates salt spray and light, sandy soil. Prefers full sun. Propagated by root division in spring. Summer-flowering.

DESCRIPTION Lavender or pink daisy-like flowers have golden yellow centers. Excellent for garden display in mixed borders and rock gardens. Good for cutting.

RECOMMENDED VARIETY Hybrids of *E. speciosus* and *E. glaucus*.

BOTANICAL NAME *Eryngium giganteum*

COMMON NAME Giant Sea-holly

RANGE Native to Mexico. Hardy zone 5 south.

HEIGHT 2 to 3 feet; upright, bushy habit.

CULTURE Prefers sandy, fertile soil in full sun. Propagated by seed. Plants die after flowering but generally self-seed. Summer-flowering.

DESCRIPTION Silver flowers resemble thistles, with a high crown surrounded by a spiky collar that is highly ornamental. Best used in mixed borders. Excellent for cutting to use in fresh and dried arrangements.

RELATED SPECIES *E. amethystinum* has steel blue flowers and is hardy from zone 2 south.

BOTANICAL NAME *Eupatorium coelestinum*

COMMON NAME Perennial Ageratum

RANGE Native to North America. Hardy zone 5 south.

HEIGHT 2 feet; bushy, spreading habit.

CULTURE Easy to grow in any well-drained soil in sun or partial shade. Propagated by seed and root division. Summer-flowering.

DESCRIPTION Fluffy flower heads are mostly powder blue. Leaves are dark green, spear shaped. Popular for mixed beds and borders. Also useful for wild gardens, either woodland or meadow.

RELATED SPECIES *E. fistulosum* ('Joe-pye Weed') with tall, 8 feet flower spikes and massive, fluffy pink flower clusters.

This perennial border in front of an old stone wall includes blue woodland phlox, silvery lamb's ear, and Siberian iris.

Mixed varieties of hostas are used here as a carefree foundation. This site is shaded during the afternoon.

BOTANICAL NAME *Euphorbia epithymoides*

COMMON NAME Cushion Spurge

RANGE Native to Europe. Hardy zone 4 south.

HEIGHT 12 inches; low, mounded habit.

CULTURE Easy to grow in any well-drained soil in full sun. Propagated mostly by root division. Drought resistant; prefers a dry summer climate. Early summer-flowering.

DESCRIPTION Creates a cushion of bright yellow flowers. Leaves are succulent, green, oval. Popular for planting among rock gardens and dry walls, also edging paths.

RELATED SPECIES *E. myrsinites* ('Myrtle Euphorbia'), has yellow flowers and prostrate, sprawling stems suitable for dry slopes. Many other species are used in perennial gardens.

BOTANICAL NAME *Gaillardia* x *grandiflora*

COMMON NAME Blanket-flower

RANGE Native to North America. Hardy zone 4 south.

HEIGHT 2 to 3 feet; erect, bushy habit.

CULTURE Prefers sandy, well-drained soil in full sun. Propagated by seed and root division. Summer-flowering.

DESCRIPTION Mostly red, daisy-like flowers with yellow petal tips. Other colors include yellow and burgundy. Gray-green leaves are deeply indented. Popular for wildflower meadows, also mixed beds and borders. Excellent cut flower. Dwarf varieties like 'Goblin' and 'Baby Cole' are suitable for rock gardens and edging.

BOTANICAL NAME *Geranium himaleyense*

COMMON NAME Blue Cranesbill

RANGE Native to the Himalayas. Hardy zone 4 south.

HEIGHT 12 inches; mounded, spreading habit.

CULTURE Easy to grow in any well-drained soil in sun or partial shade. Propagated by seed and root division. Spring- and early summer-flowering.

DESCRIPTION Gorgeous lilac blue, saucer-shaped flowers bloom profusely on light, airy foliage that is deeply serrated. Largest flowered of the cranesbill geraniums. Popular for mixed beds and borders, also rock gardens.

RECOMMENDED VARIETY 'Johnson's Blue' an extremely profuse blooming hybrid.

RELATED SPECIES *G. sanguineum* with pink or rose flowers, and *G. psilostemon* exhibiting a bushy, erect habit and rose flowers with black centers.

BOTANICAL NAME *Geum chiloense*

COMMON NAME Chilean Avens

RANGE Native to South America. Hardy zone 5 south.

HEIGHT 2 feet; erect, airy habit.

CULTURE Prefers fertile, moist, well-drained loam in sun or partial shade. Propagated by seed and root division. Early spring-flowering.

DESCRIPTION Flowers resemble miniature roses, usually semi-double in orange, red, and yellow. Leaves are deeply indented, strawberry-like. Popular for mixed beds and borders. Good for cutting.

RECOMMENDED VARIETIES 'Mrs. Bradshaw' (orange-scarlet) and 'Lady Stratheden' (yellow).

BOTANICAL NAME *Gypsophila paniculata*

COMMON NAME Baby's-breath

RANGE Native to Europe. Hardy zone 3 south.

HEIGHT 2 to 3 feet; billowing habit.

CULTURE Prefers alkaline, moist, well-drained soil in full sun. Propagated mostly by seeds. Summer-flowering.

DESCRIPTION Dainty white or pale pink flowers are borne in such profusion on brittle, slender stems, that the whole plant looks like a cloud or patch of mist. Good for garden display in mixed borders, also for cutting in fresh arrangements and as a dried flower.

RECOMMENDED VARIETIES 'Bristol Fairy' (white, double flowers) and 'Pink Fairy' (light pink, double flowers).

BOTANICAL NAME *Helianthemum nummularium*

COMMON NAME Rock Rose

RANGE Native to Europe. Hardy zone 6 south.

HEIGHT 12 inches; ground-hugging habit.

CULTURE Tolerates a wide range of soils with good drainage in full sun. Propagated mostly from seeds. Spring-flowering. ??

DESCRIPTION Spreading, evergreen plants are smothered with delicate pill-sized flowers with petals that look like crèpe paper, in yellow, orange, white, pink, and rose red. Popular for rock gardens and dry walls.

BOTANICAL NAME *Helenium autumnale*

COMMON NAME Sneezeweed

RANGE Native to North America. Hardy zone 4 south.

HEIGHT 5 feet; upright, bushy habit.

CULTURE Prefers moist, fertile, loam soil in full sun. Propagated by root division in spring. May need staking. Late summer-flowering.

DESCRIPTION Daisy-like flowers are produced in abundance on tall stems. Color range includes yellow, orange, and rusty red, some bicolored. Leaves are green, narrow, pointed. Popular for mixed beds and borders. Good for cutting.

BOTANICAL NAME *Helianthus* x *multiflorus*

COMMON NAME Perennial Sunflower

RANGE Native to North America. Hardy zone 5 south.

HEIGHT 5 to 6 feet; upright, bushy habit.

CULTURE Prefers moist, fertile, loam soil in full sun. Propagated by seed and root division. May need staking. Summer-flowering.

DESCRIPTION Golden yellow daisy-like flowers can be single or double, held high on stiff, slender stems. Leaves are dark green, spear shaped. Popular as an accent in mixed beds and borders.

RECOMMENDED VARIETY 'Flore pleno' has a full double flower. Good for cutting.

RELATED SPECIES *Helianthus angustifolius* ('Swamp Sunflower') is a familiar sight along waysides in late summer, tolerating boggy conditions.

BOTANICAL NAME *Helleborus niger*

COMMON NAME Christmas-rose

RANGE Native to Europe. Hardy zone 4 south.

HEIGHT 6 to 12 inches; low, spreading habit.

CULTURE Prefers moist, loam, or humus-rich soil in partial shade. Propagated by seed (must be fresh) and root division. Winter- and early spring-flowering.

DESCRIPTION Pure white flowers resemble single flowered roses, change to green with age, have golden yellow centers. Leaves are leathery, toothed, appear after the flowers die. Good to use in rock gardens, woodland gardens, and edging mixed beds and borders.

RELATED SPECIES *H. orientalis* ('Lenten Rose') is very similar but with a wider color range, including purple, pink, white, and cream, some with freckles.

BOTANICAL NAME *Heliopsis helianthoides*

COMMON NAME False Sunflower

RANGE Native to North America. Hardy zone 4 south.

HEIGHT 4 feet; erect, bushy habit.

CULTURE Easy to grow in any well-drained soil in full sun. Propagated by seed and root division. Late summer-flowering.

DESCRIPTION Golden yellow daisy-like flowers are mostly single and semi-double. Dark green, spear-shaped leaves. Highly popular as an accent for mixed beds and borders. Excellent for cutting.

RECOMMENDED VARIETY 'Incomparabilis' grows single and semi-double flowers.

Daylilies in an open, sunny area are framed by the branches of an ornamental crabapple tree. Hostas thrive in the shade of the apple tree.

BOTANICAL NAME *Hemerocallis* hybrids

COMMON NAME Daylilies

RANGE Developed from species native to Asia. Hardy zone 4 south.

HEIGHT 3 to 4 feet; tufted, clump-forming habit.

CULTURE Easy to grow in any well-drained garden soil in sun or partial shade. Drought tolerant. Propagated by root division. Summer-flowering.

DESCRIPTION Orange, red, yellow, mahogany, pink, and lilac blue trumpet-shaped flowers are borne on long stems. Popular as an accent in mixed beds and borders, also massed as a ground cover for erosion control of dry slopes.

RECOMMENDED VARIETIES 'Pink Dawn,' 'Hyperion' (yellow), and 'Stella di Oro' (orange).

BOTANICAL NAME *Heuchera sanguinea*

COMMON NAME Coral-bells

RANGE Native to North America. Hardy from zone 4 south.

HEIGHT 2 feet; rosette-forming habit.

CULTURE Prefers fertile, well-drained, humus-rich soil in sun or partial shade. Propagated by seed and root division. Early summer-flowering.

DESCRIPTION Tiny, red or pink bell-shaped flowers clustered at the top of slender, wiry stems, held well above the ivy-shaped leaves. Popular for rock gardens, also as accents in mixed beds and borders. Good for cutting. Heuchera has been crossed with Tiarella, ('Foamflower') a North American woodland wildflower, to produce a more spirelike hybrid called Heucharella.

BOTANICAL NAME *Hibiscus moscheutos*

COMMON NAME Rose Mallow

RANGE Native to North America. Hardy zone 5 south.

HEIGHT 4 to 5 feet; erect habit.

CULTURE Prefers moist, fertile, loam soil in full sun. Tolerates boggy conditions. Propagated mostly by seeds. May need staking. Summer-flowering.

DESCRIPTION Flowers of hybrid varieties are unusually large—the size of dinner plates—in white, crimson, and pink, many with a contrasting center. Flowers last only a day, but plants flower continuously from mid-summer to fall frost. The large green leaves are attractively heart shaped. Popular for mixed borders and edging stream banks.

RECOMMENDED VARIETIES 'Southern Belle' (blooms first year from seed sown in January or February) and 'Super Giants' (largest flowers).

BOTANICAL NAME *Hosta seiboldiana*

COMMON NAME Plantain-lily

RANGE Native to Japan. Hardy zone 4 south.

HEIGHT 2 to 3 feet; low, rosette-forming habit.

CULTURE Prefers moist, humus-rich loam soil in partial shade. Propagated by root division. Where snails or slugs are a problem, bait heavily to avoid unsightly leaf damage. Summer-flowering.

DESCRIPTION Mostly admired for its large, blue-green, paddle-shaped leaves that are heavily textured and blistered, with prominent leaf veins. Foliage turns a lovely golden color in autumn. Lilac flowers are borne on long stems high above the foliage. Popular for edging shaded walkways, also stream banks and pond margins in woodland settings.

RECOMMENDED VARIETY 'Frances William.'

RELATED SPECIES *H. fortunei*, *H. lancifolia*, and *H. undulata* are also popular perennials with different leaf colorings and leaf shapes.

BOTANICAL NAME *Iberis sempervirens*

COMMON NAME Perennial Candytuft

RANGE Native to Mediterranean. Hardy zone 4 south.

HEIGHT 12 inches; mounded, spreading habit.

CULTURE Tolerates a wide range of soils providing drainage is good. Propagated by seed and root division. Spring-flowering.

DESCRIPTION Dense, white flower clusters cover the low, ground-hugging plants. Dark green leaves are evergreen, narrow, pointed. Popular for rock gardens and dry walls; also for edging mixed beds and borders.

BOTANICAL NAME *Iris germanica*

COMMON NAME Bearded Iris

RANGE Native to Europe. Hardy zone 4 south.

HEIGHT 2 to 4 feet; upright, clump-forming habit.

CULTURE Easy to grow in any well-drained garden soil in full sun. Propagated by division of rhizomes any time of year. Blooms spring and early summer.

DESCRIPTION Slender, sword-shaped leaves emerge in spring from fleshy roots called rhizomes. Flowers are large and showy, usually featuring a prominent arching petal called a "lip" and an eye-catching yellow arrangement of stamens known as the "beard." Color range includes white, yellow, orange, pink, red, blue, purple, and black, plus bicolors. Good for mixed beds and borders, creating a temporary hedge effect. Also good for large floral arrangements. Spicy fragrance. Numerous hybrids have been created, including dwarfs suitable for rock gardens.

BOTANICAL NAME *Iris sibirica*

COMMON NAME Siberian Iris

RANGE Native to North-central Europe. Hardy zone 4 south.

HEIGHT 2 to 4 feet; upright, clump-forming habit.

CULTURE Prefers acidic, moist soil in full sun. Propagated by root division in spring or autumn. Blooms in late spring.

DESCRIPTION Long, slender leaves emerge in spring, remain decorative all summer. Flowers are numerous on tall, slender stems. Color range is mostly shades of blue and white. Good for mixed beds and borders. Especially attractive massed along stream banks and pond margins. Excellent for cutting. A number of good hybrids have expanded the color range to include yellow.

RELATED SPECIES *I. pseudacorus* ('Flag Iris'), *I. kaempferi* ('Japanese Iris'), and *I. cristata* ('Crested Iris').

BOTANICAL NAME *Kniphofia uvaria*

COMMON NAME Red-hot Poker

RANGE Native to South Africa. Hardy zone 5 south.

HEIGHT 3 to 4 feet; erect, clump-forming habit.

CULTURE Prefers fertile, well-drained loam soil in full sun. Drought resistant. Propagated mainly by root division and offsets. Summer-flowering.

DESCRIPTION Tubular flowers in red and yellow are clustered at the top of a poker-straight, thick, succulent stem held high above the leaves which are spiky, arching up and out in a clump. Popular for mixed beds and borders, also rock gardens. Excellent for cutting.

English lavender planted informally among dwarf mugo pines creates a decorative ground cover beside a patio.

BOTANICAL NAME *Lathyrus latifolius*

COMMON NAME Perennial Sweet Pea

RANGE Native to Europe. Hardy zone 4 south.

HEIGHT 6 to 9 feet; vining habit.

CULTURE Tolerates a wide range of soils providing drainage is good, in full sun. Propagated mostly by seeds. Needs staking to climb. Summer-flowering.

DESCRIPTION Easy to grow, vigorous climber with stems and flowers like Sweet Peas, but a more limited color range—mostly pink, white, and rose red. Popular for covering unsightly slopes as a ground cover and for training up posts or walls as a tall, decorative vine.

BOTANICAL NAME *Lavandula angustifolia*

COMMON NAME English Lavender

RANGE Native to Mediterranean. Hardy from zone 5 south.

HEIGHT 2 to 3 feet; mound-shaped, bushy habit.

CULTURE Easy to grow in many well-drained soils in full sun. Propagated by seed and cuttings. Summer-flowering.

DESCRIPTION Fragrant violet-blue or white flower spikes grow in abundance above billowing plants with gray-green foliage. Popular as temporary "hedges" to line walkways. Also use as accents in mixed beds and borders. Super cut flower both fresh and dried.

RECOMMENDED VARIETY 'Hidcote,' a deep blue.

BOTANICAL NAME *Liatris spicata*

COMMON NAME Bottlebrush; Gayfeather

RANGE Native to North America. Hardy from zone 4 south.

HEIGHT 4 to 5 feet; erect, bushy habit.

CULTURE Easy to grow in any well-drained garden soil in full sun. Propagated by seed and root division. Summer-flowering.

DESCRIPTION Purple or white flower spikes resemble bottle brushes, stand erect like pokers held well above the narrow-leafed foliage. Popular as an accent in mixed beds and borders. Excellent for both fresh and dried arrangements.

RECOMMENDED VARIETY 'Kobold' displays deep purple flowers.

BOTANICAL NAME *Ligularia* x *prezewalskii*

COMMON NAME Rocket Ligularia

RANGE Native to Asia. Hardy zone 4 south.

HEIGHT 6 feet; erect, spirelike habit.

CULTURE Demands a moist, humus-rich, fertile soil in partial shade. Leaves wilt as soon as soil dries out and during direct afternoon sunlight. Propagated by root division. Early summer-flowering.

DESCRIPTION Towering flower spikes are crowded with bright golden yellow flowers on slender black stems that contrast spectacularly with large, sharply indented, highly decorative leaves. Popular as a background for mixed beds and borders; also stream banks and pond margins. Good for cutting.

RECOMMENDED VARIETY 'The Rocket' with a slight bronze cast to the leaves.

BOTANICAL NAME *Lilium lancifolium*

COMMON NAME Tiger Lilies

RANGE Native to Asia. Hardy 4 south.

HEIGHT 4 to 6 feet; erect habit.

CULTURE Prefers moist, fertile, humus-rich soil in sun or partial shade. Propagated mostly by bulbils that form in the leaf axils or division of bulbous roots. May need staking. Summer-flowering.

DESCRIPTION Nodding orange flowers are exotically spotted, hang from the top of tall, slender stems. Leaves are narrow, lancelike. Naturalizes easily. Popular for backgrounds in mixed beds and borders. Excellent for cutting. There are hundreds of other related species of lilies. Also known as *L. Tigrinum*.

BOTANICAL NAME *Linum perenne*

COMMON NAME Blue Flax

RANGE Native to Europe. Hardy zone 5 south.

HEIGHT 1 to 2 feet; billowing habit.

CULTURE Easy to grow in a wide range of soils with good drainage in full sun. Propagated by seed and cuttings. Spring-flowering.

DESCRIPTION Dainty blue flowers are borne in abundance on light, airy stems with narrow leaves. Popular in mixed beds and borders, also wildflower meadows. Not a long lasting perennial, but self-seeds.

Summer phlox and globe thistle make good companions in this perennial border overlooking a formal lawn area with a summer house.

BOTANICAL NAME *Liriope muscari*

COMMON NAME Lily-turf

RANGE Native to Asia. Hardy zone 6 south.

HEIGHT 18 inches; compact, clump-forming habit.

CULTURE Prefers fertile, humus-rich loam soil in sun or partial shade. Propagated by root division. Summer-flowering.

DESCRIPTION Mostly grown for its grasslike evergreen leaves which can be dark green or variegated green and cream. Lavender-blue or white flower spikes appear among the foliage. Mostly used for edging walkways, beds, and borders. Also popular as a ground cover.

BOTANICAL NAME *Lobelia cardinalis*

COMMON NAME Scarlet Lobelia

RANGE Native to North America. Hardy zone 3 south.

HEIGHT 4 to 5 feet; erect, spirelike habit.

CULTURE Prefers moist, humus-rich, acidic soil in partial shade. Propagated by seed and root division. Tolerates boggy conditions. Summer-flowering.

DESCRIPTION Striking spires of cardinal red flowers, contrasting well with the dark green, serrated spear-shaped leaves. Plants are short-lived, but readily seed themselves. Popular in mixed beds and borders, also woodland gardens and along stream banks. Good for cutting.

A backyard perennial garden featuring a wide assortment of varieties, including 'Morden's Pink,' lythrum, white baby's-breath, purple coneflowers, 'Pinwheel' rudbeckias, and 'Alaska' shasta daisies.

This informal perennial garden situated between a porch and a busy road features white phlox, pink lythrum, yellow coreopsis, red beebalm, and orange Asiatic hybrid lilies.

BOTANICAL NAME *Lupinus* hybrids

COMMON NAME Russell Lupines

RANGE Developed in England from native North American species. Hardy zone 5 south.

HEIGHT 3 feet; erect, clump-forming habit.

CULTURE Prefers moist, sandy soil or well-drained loam. Propagated mostly from seeds. Best treated as a biennial. Self-sows easily. Spring-flowering.

DESCRIPTION Spires of fragrant, pea-like flowers are white, yellow, red, pink, blue, and purple, many bicolored. Leaves are dark green, like splayed fingers. Lupines thrive best in cool, coastal gardens since they cannot tolerate hot, dry summers. Popular for mixed beds and borders, also meadow wildflower gardens.

RELATED SPECIES: *L. perennis* (yellow flowering), native to the East Coast and the similar *L. arboreus*, native to the West Coast. Good for cutting, but flower spikes will wilt unless wired.

BOTANICAL NAME *Lychnis chalcedonica*

COMMON NAME Maltese Cross

RANGE Native to Siberia. Hardy zone 4 south.

HEIGHT 2 to 3 feet; erect habit.

CULTURE Easy to grow in any well-drained garden soil in sun or partial shade. Propagated by seed or root division. Summer-flowering.

DESCRIPTION Clusters of scarlet red flowers are borne on slender stems, each floret the shape of a Maltese cross. Leaves are dark green, spear shaped. Popular as an accent in mixed beds and borders. Excellent for cutting.

RELATED SPECIES *L. coronaria* ('Rose campion').

BOTANICAL NAME *Lysimachia punctata*

COMMON NAME Yellow Loosestrife

RANGE Native to Europe. Hardy zone 5 south.

HEIGHT 2 to 3 feet; spirelike habit.

CULTURE Prefers moist loam soil in sun or partial shade. Propagated by root division. Tolerates boggy conditions. Early summer-flowering.

DESCRIPTION Erect spikes of yellow flowers grow in clumps. Spear-shaped, ruffled green leaves. Popular as an accent in mixed beds and borders, also pond margins and stream banks.

RELATED SPECIES *L. clethroides* ('Gooseneck') has small, terminal spikes of white flowers with a curious twist at the tips. Both species are suitable for cutting.

BOTANICAL NAME *Lythrum salicaria*

COMMON NAME Purple Loosestrife

RANGE Native to North America. Hardy zone 4 south.

HEIGHT 2 to 5 feet; erect, spirelike habit.

CULTURE Prefers moist, fertile, loam soil in full sun. Tolerates boggy conditions. Propagated by root division. Summer-flowering.

DESCRIPTION Thousands of small, purple flowers are crowded along slender stems, resembling rockets. Leaves are dark green, willowlike. Popular as an accent in mixed beds and borders, also for planting along pond margins and stream banks. The wild types are a familiar sight in swampy areas, spreading across acres of marsh. Cultivated varieties do not readily naturalize.

RECOMMENDED VARIETY 'Morden's Pink' is suitable for cutting.

BOTANICAL NAME *Monarda didyma*

COMMON NAME Bee-balm; Bergamot

RANGE Native to North America. Hardy zone 4 south.

HEIGHT 3 to 4 feet; bushy habit.

CULTURE Prefers moist, fertile, loam soil in full sun. Propagated by root division in spring. Summer-flowering.

DESCRIPTION Tubular flowers emerge in a circle to make an attractive crown, borne in profusion on slender stems. Leaves are like mint, aromatic—a source of the flavoring for Earl Grey tea. Colors include red, pink, white, and purple. Popular accent for mixed beds and borders.

RECOMMENDED VARIETIES 'Cambridge Scarlet' (bright red) and 'Croftway Pink' (light pink).

RELATED SPECIES *M. fistulosa*, a wild form with fragrant pink flowers.

BOTANICAL NAME *Myosotis scorpioides*

COMMON NAME Forget-me-not

RANGE Native to Europe. Hardy zone 5 south.

HEIGHT 6 to 12 inches; low, mounded habit.

CULTURE Prefers moist, fertile, humus-rich loam soil in sun or partial shade. Propagated by seed and root division in early spring. Early spring-flowering.

DESCRIPTION Myriad, small blue flowers with yellow centers are borne in airy clusters creating a misty appearance. Leaves are paddle shaped. Popular for massing in a bed, especially among tulips. Good for edging walkways and woodland paths. Also suitable for pond margins and stream banks.

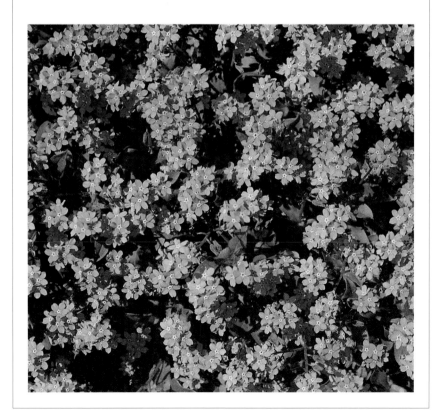

BOTANICAL NAME *Nepeta mussinii*

COMMON NAME Ornamental Catmint

RANGE Native to Europe. Hardy zone 4 south.

HEIGHT 2 to 3 feet; bushy habit.

CULTURE Prefers moist, fertile, loam soil in full sun. Propagated by seed and root division. A hybrid, *N.* x *faasenii*, does not set seed and generally produces the best flowering display. Summer-flowering.

DESCRIPTION Mintlike plants produce dense clusters of mauve blue flowers. Leaves are dark green, heart-shaped. Creates a hedge effect and therefore is popular for lining walkways. Also used in mixed beds and borders.

RELATED SPECIES *N. cataria*, ('Catmint'). These plants attract cats.

BOTANICAL NAME *Oenothera tetragona*

COMMON NAME Sundrop

RANGE Native to North America. Hardy zone 5 south.

HEIGHT 18 to 24 inches; upright, clump-forming habit.

CULTURE Prefers sandy or well-drained loam soil in full sun. Propagated by root division. Early summer-flowering.

DESCRIPTION Cup-shaped yellow flowers shimmer like satin. Leaves are green, spear shaped. Popular for mixed beds and borders. Forms a dense, spreading mass of brilliant yellow.

RELATED SPECIES The taller *O. missourensis* ('Evening Primrose') and pink-flowered *O. speciosa* 'Texas Wine Cup'.

BOTANICAL NAME *Opuntia humifusa*

COMMON NAME Hardy Prickly-pear

RANGE Native to North America. Hardy zone 5 south.

HEIGHT 6 inches; prostrate, ground-hugging habit.

CULTURE Easy to grow in any well-drained garden soil in full sun. Propagated by rooting the leaves (pads) in moist sand. Drought resistant. Early summer-flowering.

DESCRIPTION This true cactus has oblong pads bristling with sharp spines, producing shimmering yellow flowers up to 3 inches across. When the flowers die, the plant's edible red fruits develop and ripen in autumn. Popular for rock gardens and dry walls.

BOTANICAL NAME *Paeonia officinalis*

COMMON NAME Herbaceous Peony

RANGE Native to Europe and Asia. Hardy zone 5 south.

HEIGHT 3 to 4 feet; bushy habit.

CULTURE Prefers cool, moist, humus-rich loam soil that drains well. Best in full sun. Propagated by root division. Blooms in late spring.

DESCRIPTION Handsome shrublike plants have large single and double flowers up to 6 inches across in white, pink, and red. Leaves are dark green, deeply indented. Good accent in mixed beds or borders; also planted en masse as a hedge. Good for cutting.

RECOMMENDED VARIETIES 'Estate Hybrids' developed by an Illinois peony breeder.

BOTANICAL NAME *Paeonia suffruticosa*

COMMON NAME Tree Peony

RANGE Native to China and Japan. Hardy zone 5 south.

HEIGHT 4 to 6 feet; bushy, shrublike habit.

CULTURE Prefers cool, moist, humus-rich, loam soil in a sheltered, well-drained location. Tolerates light shade. Propagated by root division and stem cuttings. Heavy feeders, they need a high-phosphorus soil content. Spring-flowering.

DESCRIPTION Spectacularly large single and double flowers measure up to 10 inches across in white, yellow, red, pink, and deep crimson. Popular as an accent in mixed beds and borders. Older plants form woody stems that can be artistically shaped. Excellent cut flower. Handsome, indented green foliage also popular with flower arrangers.

BOTANICAL NAME *Papaver orientale*

COMMON NAME Oriental Poppy

RANGE Native to Asia. Hardy zone 4 south.

HEIGHT 3 to 4 feet; upright habit.

CULTURE Easy to grow in any well-drained garden soil in full sun. Propagated by seed and root division. Blooms in spring.

DESCRIPTION Shimmering satinlike flowers up to 10 inches across, single- and double-flowered, with a mass of powdery black stamens at the center. Colors include red, orange, pink, purple, and white, mostly with attractive black blotches at the petal base. Leaves are green, fernlike, and hairy. Popular for mixed beds and borders, or massed alone. Striking cut flower if ends are quickly scorched or boiled to prevent wilting.

Here, a formal border is accented with spring-flowering perennials, including white tree peonies, blue woodland phlox, tulips, and yellow poppies.

BOTANICAL NAME *Perovskia atripicifolia*

COMMON NAME Russian Sage

RANGE Native to Asia. Hardy zone 5 south.

HEIGHT 3 to 4 feet; upright, shrubby habit.

CULTURE Easy to grow in any well-drained garden soil in full sun. Propagated by cuttings taken in summer. Summer-flowering.

DESCRIPTION Small blue flowers form showy spikes. Twiggy stems have small, narrow gray leaves which when bruised are highly aromatic. A good background in mixed beds and borders. Excellent cut flower, both fresh and dried.

BOTANICAL NAME *Phlox paniculata*

COMMON NAME Summer Phlox

RANGE Native to North America. Hardy zone 4 south.

HEIGHT 3 to 4 feet; upright habit.

CULTURE Prefers deeply cultivated, fertile loam soil in full sun. Propagated by seed and root division. Susceptible to powdery mildew controlled by fungicidal spray. May need staking. Summer-flowering.

DESCRIPTION Bold flower clusters grow to 9 inches long in white and shades of red, pink, salmon, lavender, and blue. Good for tall backgrounds in mixed borders. Popular for cutting. 'Pinafore' is an excellent dwarf with clear pink flowers.

BOTANICAL NAME *Phlox subulata*

COMMON NAME Moss-pinks

RANGE Native to North America. Hardy zone 4 south.

HEIGHT 6 inches; low, ground-hugging habit.

CULTURE Requires excellent drainage and full sun. Propagated by seed and root division. Spring-flowering.

DESCRIPTION Small, star-shaped flowers are crowded closely together to form a cushion of color in pink, red, blue, and white. Narrow, gray-green leaves are evergreen. Good for rock gardens and dry walls. Creates an attractive ground cover when planted in a mass. Useful for edging beds and borders.

BOTANICAL NAME *Physalis alkekengi*

COMMON NAME Chinese Lanterns

RANGE Native to the Orient. Hardy zone 5 south.

HEIGHT 2 feet; spreading, sprawling habit.

CULTURE Tolerates poor soil, providing drainage is good, in full sun. Propagated mostly by seed and division of its invasive underground roots. Late-summer flowering.

DESCRIPTION Inconspicuous, cream colored star-shaped flowers are replaced by ornamental lantern-shaped seed cases that turn orange-red in late summer. Leaves are spear shaped. Generally grown massed in a bed by themselves. The stems are best gathered in autumn, air-dried and used for cheerful, long-lasting dried arrangements during winter months. Also known as *P. franchetii*.

BOTANICAL NAME *Physostegia virginiana*

COMMON NAME Obedient Plant

RANGE Native to North America. Hardy zone 4 south.

HEIGHT 3 to 5 feet; upright, clump forming habit.

CULTURE Prefers moist soil, full sun. Propagated by seed and root division. Late summer-flowering.

DESCRIPTION Pink or white flowers resemble Snapdragons, form spikes at the top of long, slender stems. Leaves are narrow, pointed. A member of the mint family, the stems are square. Good for late-flowering garden display in mixed beds and borders. Spreading roots may need thinning each year to prevent them from becoming invasive. Called 'Obedient Plant' because flower heads can be twisted into different positions.

BOTANICAL NAME *Platycodon grandiflorus*

COMMON NAME Balloonflower

RANGE Native to China. Hardy zone 4 south.

HEIGHT 2 feet; upright habit.

CULTURE Prefers acidic, loam, fertile soil in full sun or partial shade. Propagated by seeds. Blooms in summer.

DESCRIPTION Beautiful, clear blue bell-shaped flowers up to 3 inches across on erect stems. White and pink forms, double and semi-double are also available. Leaves are narrow, pointed. Gets its common name, 'Balloonflower', from the appearance of inflated flower buds. Excellent for mixed beds and borders and for rock gardens. Good for cutting.

BOTANICAL NAME *Polemonium reptans*

COMMON NAME Jacob's-ladder

RANGE Native to North America. Hardy zone 4 south.

HEIGHT 12 inches; low, spreading habit.

CULTURE Prefers moist, humus-rich, loam soil in sun or partial shade. Propagated by root division in spring. Spring-flowering.

DESCRIPTION Small, light blue bell-shaped flowers are crowded in loose clusters. Leaves are made up of oval leaflets symmetrically arranged like a ladder. Useful for edging walkways and as a ground cover in woodland gardens.

RELATED SPECIES *P. caeruleum,* taller growing (to 3 feet) and useful as a border accent.

BOTANICAL NAME *Polygonum bistorta*

COMMON NAME Knotweed

RANGE Native to Europe. Hardy zone 4 south.

HEIGHT 2 to 3 feet; erect, clump-forming habit.

CULTURE Prefers moist, fertile, loam soil in partial shade. Propagated by seed, cuttings, and root division. Summer-flowering.

DESCRIPTION Pokerlike pink flowers are held well above the green, straplike foliage. Popular for mixed beds and borders, particularly as an edging. Good for cutting.

RECOMMENDED VARIETY 'Superbum' with extra large flowers.

A beautiful planting of Japanese primulas thrive in boggy soil along the banks of a stream at Winterthur Gardens, Wilmington, Delaware.

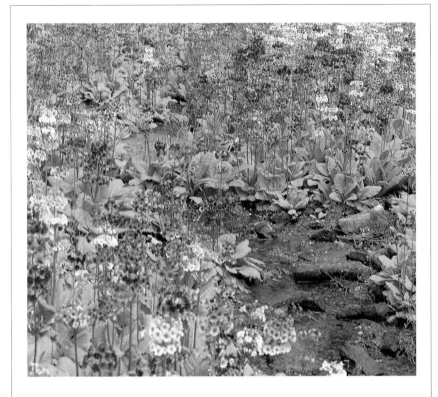

BOTANICAL NAME *Primula japonica*

COMMON NAME Japanese Primrose; Candelabra Primrose

RANGE Native to China and Japan. Hardy zone 6 south.

HEIGHT 1 to 2 feet; rosette-forming habit.

CULTURE Prefers moist, acidic, humus-rich soil in light shade. Propagated by seed and root division. Blooms in spring.

DESCRIPTION Plants form dark green clumps of succulent crinkled, veined leaves. Flowers are borne in clusters on slender stems. Colors include white, red, pink, and purple. Good for massing along stream banks, pond margins, and wherever soil remains moist all year.

RELATED SPECIES *P. beesianum* ('Bees Primrose') has yellow and orange flowers. Cannot tolerate hot or dry summers.

BOTANICAL NAME *Primula x polyantha*

COMMON NAME Polyantha Primrose

RANGE A hybrid species native to Europe. Hardy zone 5 south.

HEIGHT 12 inches; rosette-forming habit.

CULTURE Prefers moist, acidic, humus-rich soil in partial shade. Propagated by seed and root division. Blooms in spring.

DESCRIPTION Primrose-like flowers are borne in clusters on slender stems. Color range includes yellow, red, white, and blue. Leaves are fleshy, green, crinkled. Excellent for shade gardens, especially in woodland. 'Pacific Giants' have the largest flowers and widest color range, though not long-lived.

RELATED SPECIES *P. vulgaris* ('English Primrose') and *P. veris* ('Cowslip').

Black-eyed Susans, purple coneflowers, and orange daylilies decorate a property boundary.

BOTANICAL NAME *Pyrethrum roseum*

COMMON NAME Painted Daisy

RANGE Native to Mediterranean. Hardy zone 4 south.

HEIGHT 2 feet; upright, clump-forming habit.

CULTURE Prefers moist, fertile, loam soil in full sun. Propagated by seed and root division. Spring- and early summer-flowering.

DESCRIPTION Single and double daisy-like flowers in white, pink, rose, red, and crimson, with contrasting yellow centers. The flowers are borne on stiff stems; leaves are gray-green, finely toothed. Good for mixed beds and borders. One of the very best cut flowers.

BOTANICAL NAME *Rudbeckia fulgida*

COMMON NAME Black-eyed Susans

RANGE Native to North America. Hardy zone 4 south.

HEIGHT 2 to 3 feet; upright habit.

CULTURE Easy to grow even in poor soils. Prefers moist, loam soil in full sun. Propagated by seed and root division in early spring. Summer-flowering.

DESCRIPTION Yellow, daisy-like flowers have dark brown centers up to 3 inches wide, produced in profusion. Leaves are gray-green, pointed, and narrow. Good for meadow gardens, mixed beds and borders.

RECOMMENDED VARIETY 'Goldsturm,' a compact form that produces an especially brilliant floral display.

BOTANICAL NAME *Salvia* x *superba*

COMMON NAME Violet Sage

RANGE A hybrid of species native to Europe. Hardy zone 5 south.

HEIGHT 2 feet; upright, spreading habit.

CULTURE Prefers sandy, fertile soil in full sun or light shade. Propagated by root division. Blooms in summer.

DESCRIPTION Violet-blue flowers are borne on long spikes, densely crowded together, making a strong display in mixed borders or massed alone in beds. Slender stems have narrow pointed leaves.

RECOMMENDED VARIETY 'East Friesland.'

RELATED SPECIES *S. farinacea* ('Mealy-Cup Sage') with blue and white flowers; *S. pratensis* ('Meadow Clary') with lavender blue flowers.

BOTANICAL NAME *Saponaria ocymoides*

COMMON NAME Soapwort

RANGE Native to Europe. Hardy zone 4 south.

HEIGHT 6 inches; low, ground-hugging habit.

CULTURE Easy to grow in any well-drained soil in sun or partial shade. Drought resistant. Propagated by seed and root division. Spring-flowering.

DESCRIPTION Dainty, bright pink star-shaped flowers are produced in profusion on trailing plants. Dark green lance-shaped leaves are small, pointed. Excellent choice for rock gardens and dry walls.

BOTANICAL NAME *Scabiosa caucasica*

COMMON NAME Pincushion Flower

RANGE Native to Europe. Hardy zone 4 south.

HEIGHT 3 feet; upright, spreading habit.

CULTURE Easy to grow in any well-drained garden soil in full sun. Propagated by seed or root division. May need staking. Summer-flowering.

DESCRIPTION The flat, ruffled blue flowers have a pale crest in the center, held erect on long, slender stems. Leaves are narrow, indented. Popular as an accent in mixed beds and borders. Superb for cutting.

BOTANICAL NAME *Sedum spectabile*

COMMON NAME Stonecrop

RANGE Native to China and Japan. Hardy zone 4 south.

HEIGHT 2 feet; upright, clump-forming habit.

CULTURE Tolerates poor soil, but prefers fertile loam in full sun. Drought resistant. Propagated by cuttings and root division. Late summer-flowering.

DESCRIPTION Bright pink flower clusters are flattened, circular. The individual star-shaped flowers are small, but are crowded together in a tight mass up to 6 inches wide. Leaves are blue-gray, succulent, smooth, and pointed. Plants are excellent for garden display in mixed borders and rock gardens or massed alone in beds. 'Autumn Joy,' a hybrid of *S. spectabile*, has deep, rosy red flowers that turn bronze when they die. Color will persist in a dried state well into winter, making this a valued plant for dried-flower arrangements.

BOTANICAL NAME *Stokesia laevis*

COMMON NAME Stoke's Aster

RANGE Native to North America. Hardy zone 5 south.

HEIGHT 2 feet; bushy, spreading habit.

CULTURE Easy to grow in any well-drained garden soil in sun or partial shade. Propagated by seed or root division. Spring-flowering.

DESCRIPTION Powder blue flowers resemble giant Cornflowers, up to 4 inches across. Leaves are narrow and serrated like China Asters. Good for mixed beds and borders. Suitable for cutting.

BOTANICAL NAME *Trollius europaeus*

COMMON NAME Globeflower

RANGE Native to Europe. Hardy zone 5 south.

HEIGHT 2 feet; upright, clump-forming habit.

CULTURE Prefers moist, fertile, humus-rich loam soil in sun or partial shade. Tolerates boggy conditions. Propagated by seed or root division. Spring-flowering.

DESCRIPTION Buttercup yellow globular flowers are borne erect on slender stems. Leaves are dark green, serrated. Popular for stream banks and pond margins. Suitable for cutting.

Hardy perennial yucca creates a spectacular garden highlight when covered in snow.

BOTANICAL NAME *Veronica longifolia*

COMMON NAME Speedwell

RANGE Native to Europe. Hardy zone 4 south.

HEIGHT 3 feet; erect, bushy habit.

CULTURE Easy to grow in any well-drained garden soil in full sun. Propagated by seed and root division. May need staking. Early summer-flowering.

DESCRIPTION Elegant spires of blue, white, or pink flowers. Leaves lance-like, dark green. Popular accent for mixed beds and borders.

RECOMMENDED VARIETIES 'Blue Spires,' 'White Icicle,' and 'Red Fox,' (which is actually a deep pink).

RELATED SPECIES *V. teucrium*, a dwarf, compact plant with bright blue flowers.

BOTANICAL NAME *Viola* tricolors

COMMON NAME Johnny Jump-Ups

RANGE Native to Europe. Hardy zone 5 south.

HEIGHT 6 inches; compact, bushy habit.

CULTURE Prefers moist, fertile, humus-rich soil with good drainage, in sun or partial shade. Propagated by seed and root division. Spring-flowering.

DESCRIPTION Miniature pansy-like flowers produced in abundance. Color range includes violet, white, red, and yellow, with bicolors and tricolors. Dark green leaves are narrow, pointed. Extremely popular for combining with flowering bulbs in mixed beds; also good for edging borders and as mass plantings.

RECOMMENDED VARIETY 'Helen Mount' sporting cheerfully tricolored flowers in yellow, maroon, and lavender.

BOTANICAL NAME *Yucca filamentosa*

COMMON NAME Spanish Dagger; Adam's Needle

RANGE Native to Mexico and southern U.S. Hardy zone 5 east.

HEIGHT 6 feet; spiky, clump-forming habit.

CULTURE Easy to grow in any well-drained soil in full sun. Drought tolerant. Propagated by division of offsets. Summer-flowering.

DESCRIPTION Each clump of spiny leaves sends up a flower spike resembling a huge asparagus spear, which opens out into a fountain of creamy white flowers. The leaves have nasty points as sharp as nails. Plants are best used as accents at the back of beds and borders. Also popular massed together on dry slopes for erosion control and in rock gardens. The flowers are edible in salads and taste like Belgian endive. Variegated forms with golden stripes are available, such as 'Golden Sword.'

RELATED SPECIES *Y. glauca* ('Soapweed') has narrower leaves and is more ornamental when used in containers.

CHAPTER FOUR

GARDEN PLANS

The following garden plans show some particularly effective uses for perennials. These plans are offered mostly as suggestions. They are easily adapted to suit your specific needs. Of course, the variety recommendations can also be changed to your personal preferences.

The most common use of perennials is to create a sunny border, usually with a fence, hedge, or wall in the background, at the edge of the lawn. Because of the popularity of this planting scheme, a conception planting plan covering the three main flowering periods—Spring, early Summer, and late Summer—is given so that there will be something in flower for a period of about ten weeks, extending from spring until early autumn.

There are earlier-flowering perennials—such as *Helleborus niger* and *Bergenia cordifolia*—both of which may bloom even before the last snowfalls of winter—but generally you cannot make a bold color border with these early-flowering species. Similarly, there are perennials whose colors extend into late fall and early winter, particularly among some of the ornamental grasses that produce spectacular dried flower heads (such as *Cortaderia selloana* and *Sedum* 'Autumn Joy', which carries its dried flower heads until Christmas, even in the north). Generally, however, the bold, splashy, flowering displays we associate with perennials dwindles dramatically with the first fall frost.

SPRING PERENNIAL BORDER

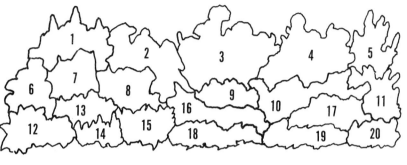

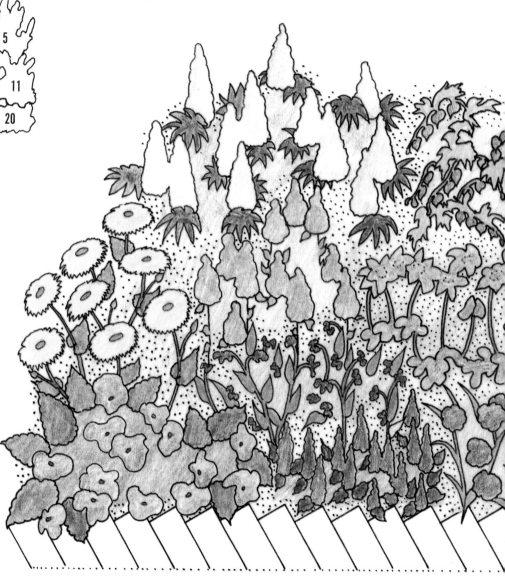

1- *Lupinus* hybrids
2- *Dicentra spectabilis*
3- *Papaver orientale*
4- *Paeonia officinalis*
5- *Baptisia australis*
6- *Doronicum cordatum*
7- *Amsonia tabernaemontana*
8- *Aquilegia* x *hybrida*
9- *Trollius europaeus*
10- *Geum chiloense*

11- *Primula* species
12- *Viola cornuta*
13- *Polygonatum commutatum*
14- *Ajuga reptans*
15- *Armeria maritima*
16- *Dianthus plumarius*
17- *Iberis sempervirens*
18- *Phlox subulata*
19- *Aurinia saxatilis*
20- *Myosotis sylvatica*

Other perennials not represented here, but that also look wonderful in a spring perennial border are: *Achillea tomentosa, Aubrieta deltoida, Bergenia cordifolia, Caltha palustris, Dictamnus albus, Digitalis* species, *Euphorbia epithymoides, Geranium sanguineum, Helleborus niger,* and *Penstemon hartwegii.*

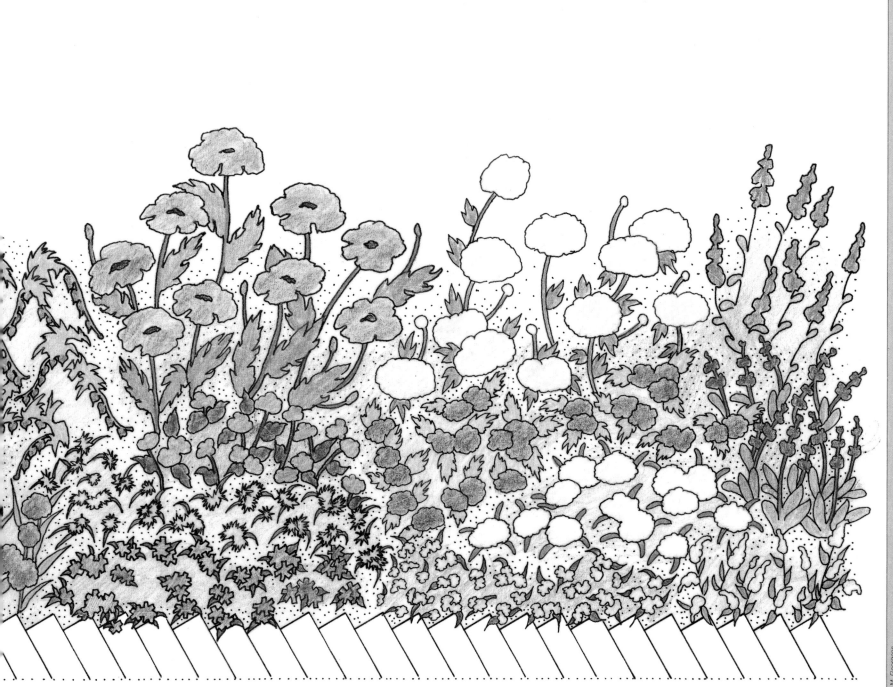

A. M. Georgens

EARLY SUMMER PERENNIAL BORDER

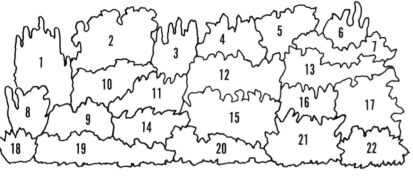

1- *Digitalis*
2- *Lilium* hybrids
3- *Cimicifuga racemosa*
4- *Delphinum elatum*
5- *Hibiscus mosceheutos*
6- *Lythrum salicaria*
7- *Phlox paniculata*
8- *Iris sibirica*
9- *Astilbe* hybrids
10- *Chrysanthemum parthenium*
11- *Kniphofia uvaria*
12- *Iris kaempferi*

13- *Monarda didyma*
14- *Rudbeckia hirta*
15- *Hemerocallis* hybrids
16- *Liatris spicata*
17- *Echinacea purpurea*
18- *Yucca filimentosa*
19- *Coreopsis lanceolata*
    or *Coreopsis verticillata*
20- *Gaillardia* x *grandiflora*
21- *Hosta seiboldiana*
22- *Liriope muscari*

Other perennials not represented here, but that are also good in an early-summer perennial border include: *Alchemilla vulgaris, Anchusa azurea, Anthemis tinctoria, Asclepias tuberosa, Astilbe* hybrids, *Campanula* species, *Echinopsis ritro, Filipendula rubra, Gypsophila paniculata, Heliopsis helianthoides, Heuchera sanguinea, Lychnis chalcedonica, Lysimachia punctata, Salvia pratensis, Scabiosa caucasica, Stachys olympia, Stokesia laevis, Tradescantia virgiana,* and the *Veronica* species.

A. M. Georgens

Late Summer Perennial Border

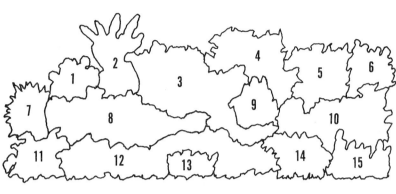

1- *Anemone japonica*
2- *Cortadera selloana*
3- *Aster Novae-anglae*
4- *Helianthus decapetalus*
5- *Helenium autumnale*
6- *Eupatorium fistulosum*
7- *Miscanthus sinensis* (grass)
8- *Sedum* 'Autumn Joy'

9- *Physostegia virginiana*
10- *Sedum spectabile*
11- *Physalis alkekengi*
12- *Chrysanthemum morifolium*
13- *Artemesia* 'Silver Mound'
14- *Pennisetum sectaceum*
15- *Stachys lanata*

Other perennials not represented here, but that will look wonderful in a late-summer perennial border include: *Hosta* hybrids and *Solidago* hybrids.

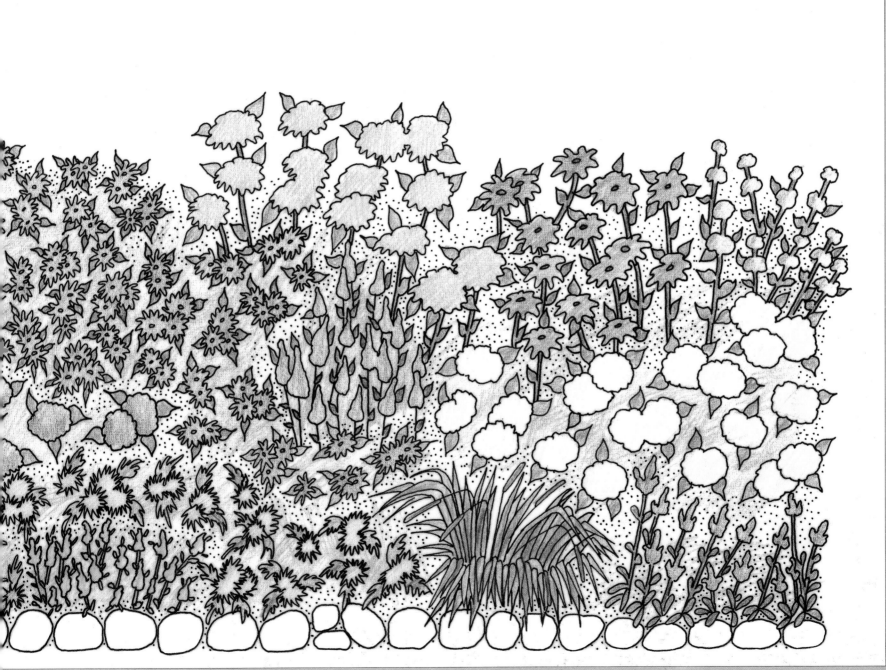

A. M. Georgens

CHAPTER FIVE

PLANT SELECTION GUIDE

Whether your garden is in the sun or the shade, your soil moist or dry, whether you prefer a cutting garden or a display garden that will be the envy of your neighborhood, there are perennial plants to suit every need. The following lists are intended as a helpful, easy reference. They are not all-inclusive, and by consulting specialist catalogs you will be able to find additions to these lists. Throughout this section, unless otherwise noted, any member of the species can be used. Or, check the encyclopedia section (Chapter Three) for specific varieties.

PERENNIALS FOR CUTTING

Achillea	*Aquilegia*
Aconitum	*Artemesia*
Agapanthus	*Asclepias*
Allium	*Aster*
Anaphalis	*Astilbe*
Anchusa	*Babtisia*
Anemone hybrida	*Belamcanda*

Anthemis	*Campanula* species
Catananche	*Kniphofia*
Centranthus	*Lavandula*
Chrysanthemum species	*Liatris*
Cimicifuga	*Lilium* species
Coreopsis	*Limonium latifolium*
Delphinium	*Lychnis*
Dianthus	*Lysimachia*
Doronicum	*Lythrum salicaria*
Echinacea	*Monarda*
Echinops	*Paeonia*
Eryngium	*Papaver* species
Eupatorium	*Penstemon*
Gaillardia	*Phlox paniculata*
Gypsophila	*Physostegia virginiana*
Helenium	*Pyrethrum*
Helianthus	*Rudbeckia*
Heliopsis	*Salvia farinacea*
Heuchera	*Scabiosa caucasica*
Iris germanica	*Stokesia*
Iris sibirica	*Veronica*

Right: Blue mountain phlox (foreground), yellow alyssum, and blue forget-me-nots (background) create sweeps of color in spring, while white flowering dogwoods carry color high into the sky.

Opposite page: Straw-colored flower plumes of feather reed grass and golden yellow rudbeckia are star performers in this meadow garden.

PERENNIALS FOR MEADOW GARDENS

Alcea
Achillea
Anthemis
Asclepias
Aster species
Baptisia
Catananche
Chrysanthemum superbum
Coreopsis
Echinacea
Eupatorium
Gaillardia
Gyposphila
Helenium
Helianthus
Heliopsis
Hemerocallis
Hibiscus
Iris sibirica
Liatris
Lilium species
Lupinus
Lythrum
Monarda
Papaver
Phlox species
Pyrethrum
Rudbeckia

PERENNIALS FOR ROCK GARDENS

Aegopodium

Ajuga

Alchemilla

Anemone pulsatilla

Anthemis

Aquilegia

Arabis

Armeria

Aubrietia

Aurinia

Bergenia

Campanula (dwarf species)

Cerastium

Dianthus

Dicentra (dwarf species)

Doronicum

Erigeron

Euphorbia (dwarf species)

Geranium (dwarf species)

Heuchera

Iberis

Lavandula

Linum

Liriope

Nepeta

Oenothera

Opuntia

Phlox subulata

Platycodon

Polygonum

Saponaria

Sedum

Stokesia

Veronica species

Viola

Yucca

Opposite page: This small city sidewalk perennial border features a handsome clump of pink stonecrop sedum, plus plantings of hosta, rudbeckia, and gaillardia; annual alyssum is used as an edging.

Left: The main components of this early spring perennial border are sky blue forget-me-nots, pale blue woodland phlox, and yellow alyssum.

A mass planting of primula japonica flowers spectacularly in a swampy area at the Leonard Buck Rock Garden, Far Hills, New Jersey.

PERENNIALS FOR DAMP AND MOIST PLACES

*Asterisked varieties will grow in permanently moist soil.

Alchemilla	Lysimachia punctata
Arum	Lythrum
Astilbe	Myosotis
*Caltha	*Nymphaea species
Eupatorium	Polygonum
Hosta	Primula japonica
Helenium	Rodgersia
Hibiscus moscheutos	Tradescantia virginiana
Iris sibirica	Trollius
*Iris pseudacorus	Zantedeschia aethiopica
Ligularia	
Lobelia cardinalis	
*Lotus	

PERENNIALS FOR FOLIAGE EFFECTS

Acanthus (indented, large, glossy leaves)
Aegopodium (silver, variegated, ivylike leaves)
Ajuga (especially purple-foliaged kinds)
Artemesia ('Silver King' has slender, silvery leaves)
Arum (mottled, glossy green and silver, arrow-shaped leaves)
Bergenia (large, ruffled, begonialike leaves)
Cerastium (silvery foliage)
Dianthus (silvery, grasslike leaves)
Epimedium (layers of heart-shaped leaves with chestnut and green zones)
Hosta (paddle-shaped leaves, some heavily savoyed)
Iris pallida (ivory-and-blue sword-shaped leaves)
Liriope (arching, evergreen straplike leaves)
Yucca filamentosa (spiky, upright leaves)

PERENNIALS FOR WOODLAND GARDENS

Aquilegia	*Iris cristata*
Arum	*Lilium* species
Astilbe	*Lobelia cardinalis*
Bergenia	*Myosotis*
Cimicifuga	*Phlox divaricata*
Dicentra	*Polemonium*
Digitalis	*Primula*
Helleborus	*Viola cornuta*
Hosta	

Opposite page: Blue-foliaged hosta seiboldi and white-spired cimifuga racemosa are good companions in this mixed border that also uses shrubs and annuals for dramatic impact.

Left: White trumpet lilies and rosy red lychnis coronaria bloom together in early summer.

Right: Hostas and hardy ferns are top choices for shady places.

Opposite page: This exquisite Victorian-style fern garden features both tender and hardy kinds in a small conservatory at the Morris Arboretum.

PERENNIAL FERN GARDEN

The following popular and easy-to-grow ferns are readily available through specialist perennial growers. Ferns are especially valuable for shade gardens and wherever cool, moist conditions prevail, such as surrounding a pool or beside a stream.

Those marked with an asterisk are tender; others are hardy to frost.

Adiantum pedatum
(Maidenhair fern)
*Asplenium nidus-avis
(Bird's nest fern)
Asplenium platyneuron
(Ebony spleenwort)
Athyrium filix-femina
(Lady fern)
*Cyrtomium falcatum
(Holly fern)
Dennstaedtia punctilobula
(Hay-scented fern)
*Dicksonia antartica
(Australian tree fern)

Dryopteris erythrosora
(Japanese sword fern)
Matteuccia Struthiopteris pensylvanica (Ostrich fern)
Osmunda cinnamomea
(Cinnamon fern)
Polypodium virginianum
(Polypody fern)
Polystichum acrostichoides
(Christmas fern)
*Woodwardia species
(Chain ferns)

PERENNIALS FOR SHADE

Adonis amurensis
Aquilegia canadensis
Brunnera macrophylla
Chrysogonum virginianum
Cimicifuga
Dicentra
Epimedium
Geranium maculatum
Helleborus
Hosta
Lobelia cardinalis

Liriope
Meconopsis cambrica
Mertensia virginica
Phlox divaricata
Polemonium
Primula vulgaris
Pulmonaria
Sanguinaria canadensis
Tiarella cordifolia
Trillium grandiflorum
Vinca minor
Viola species

(See also list of recommended ferns)

Opposite page: Bleeding hearts are excellent flowering perennials for light shade.
Left: A beautiful border of hostas create a good ornamental ground cover for the shady side of a house.

Right: A variegated form of pampas plume, called 'Gold Stripe,' creates an appealing fountain effect with its arching, narrow leaves.

Opposite page: A close-up view of ribbon grass shows beautiful bands of green and white along the leaf blades, creating a decorative effect in perennial borders from spring until fall frosts.

PERENNIAL GRASSES

Ornamental grass gardens have become extremely popular in recent years, particularly in places that are exposed to high winds and places which are difficult to plant such as the prairie states and seashore. The following list of plants is readily available from specialist perennial mail-order houses.

Briza media
Calamagrostis acutiflora stricta
Cortadera selloana
Deschampsia caespitosa
Elymus glaucus
Erianthus ravennae
Festuca ovina 'glauca'
Glyceria maxima 'variegata'
Imperata cylindra rubra

Miscanthus sinensis
Miscanthus sinensis 'Gracillimus'
Miscanthus sinensis 'Zebrinus'
Panicum virgatum
Pennisetum alopecuroides
Pennisetum setaceum
Pennisetum villosum
Phalaris arundinacea picta

Right: This early spring perennial border features a mass planting of mountain phlox as a ground cover.
Opposite page: Sedum 'Autumn Joy' is not only a reliable drought-tolerant plant, its flower clusters remain decorative well into autumn.

PERENNIALS FOR GROUND COVER

Achillea tomentosa	Hosta
Aegopodium	Iberis sempervirens
Ajuga	Iris cristata
Alchemilla	Lamium
Armeria	Liriope
Artemisia schmidtiana	Lysimachia nummularia
Asperula odorata	Myosotis
Bergenia	Ophiopogon
Cerastium	Opuntia
Ceratostigma	Phlox subulata
plumbaginoides	Sedum species
Chrysogonum virginianum	Sempervivum
Coronilla varia	Stachys byzantina
Dianthus deltoides	Thymus serpyllum
Duchesnea indica	Vinca minor
Festuca ovina glauca	

PERENNIALS FOR HOT, DRY SOIL

Achillea	Gaillardia
Anthemis	Gypsophila
Arabis	Helianthemum
Artemisia	Hemerocallis
Asclepias	Iberis
Aurinia	Kniphofia
Campanula persicifolia	Lavandula
Catananche	Liatris
Cerastium tomentosum	Linum perenne
Coreopsis	Lychnis
Dianthus plumarius	Opuntia
Echinacea purpurea	Sedum species
Echinops	Veronica
Eryngium	Yucca
Euphorbia	

RED PERENNIALS

Althaea
Achillea
Aquilegia
Armeria
Arum (berries)
Asclepias
Aster
Astilbe
Aubrieta
Bergenia
Centranthus
Chrystanthemum morifolium
Dianthus
Digitalis
Erigeron
Gaillardia
Geranium species
Helenium

Hemerocallis
Heuchera
Hibiscus
Iris germanica
Kniphofia
Liatris
Lilium species
Lobelia cardinalis
Lupinus
Lychnis
Monarda
Paeonia
Papaver
Phlox paniculata
Phlox subulata
Primula polyantha
Pryethrum
Viola cornuta

PINK PERENNIALS

Althaea	Heuchera
Anemone japonica	Hibiscus
Aquilegia	Iris germanica
Armeria	Lathyrus
Aster	Liatris
Astilbe	Lilium species
Aubrieta	Liriope
Bergenia	Lupinus
Campanula species	Lythrum
Centranthus	Monarda
Chrysanthemum morifolium	Myosotis
Delphinium	Paeonia
Dianthus	Papaver
Dicentra	Phlox paniculata
Digitalis	Phlox subulata
Echinacea	Physostegia
Erigeron	Primula japonica
Eupatorium	Primula polyantha
Geranium species	Pyrethrum
Gypsophila	Saponaria
Helianthemum	Sedum spectabile
Helleborus species	Veronica

Opposite page: This woodland garden uses sky blue forget-me-nots, yellow alyssum, and pale blue woodland phlox to create color low to the ground, under a canopy of flowering dogwoods.
Left: A single plant of hollyhock makes a good structural highlight against a dry wall.

Right: This Colonial-style perennial garden, featuring yellow yarrow, purple foxglove, and blue delphinium, includes a gazebo as a strong design element.

Opposite page: A portion of the Iris Garden at Ladew Topiary Gardens, near Monkton, Maryland, uses mostly bearded iris, plus a variegated form of lily turf for edging.

BLUE PERENNIALS

Amsonia
Anemone pulsatilla
Ajuga
Acanthus
Anchusa
Aquilegia
Aster
Baptisia
Campanula
Catananche
Delphinium
Echinops
Eryngium
Geranium species
Hosta
Iris germanica
Iris sibirica
Lavandula

Linum perenne
Liriope
Lobelia siphilitica
Lupinus
Myosotis
Nepeta
Perovskia
Phlox divaricata
Phlox subulata
Platycodon
Polemonium
Primula polyantha
Salvia superba
Scabiosa
Stokesia
Veronica
Viola cornuta

WHITE PERENNIALS
(INCLUDING SILVER-FOLIAGED)

Acanthus	*Gypsophila*
Aegopodium	*Helleborus*
Ajuga reptans	*Hemerocallis*
Alcea	*Heuchera*
Amsonia	*Hosta*
Anchusa	*Iberis*
Anemone japonica	*Iris germanica*
Aquilegia	*Iris sibirica*
Arabis	*Lavandula*
Artemesia	*Liatris*
Aster	*Lilium* species
Astilbe	*Liriope*
Aubrieta	*Paeonia*
Campanula	*Phlox paniculata*
Centranthus	*Phlox subulata*
Chrysanthemum morfolium	*Physostegia*
Chrysanthemum parthenium	*Platycodon*
Chrysanthemum superbum	*Polygonum*
Cimicifuga	*Pyrethrum*
Delphinium	*Primula polyanthus*
Dicentra	*Stokesia*
Digitalis	*Veronica*
Echinacea	*Viola cornuta*
Eryngium	*Yucca*

YELLOW AND ORANGE PERENNIALS

Althaea	*Helenium*
Alchemilla	*Helianthus*
Aegopodium	*Heliopsis*
Achillea	*Hemerocallis*
Anthemis	*Iris germanica*
Aquilegia	*Iris pseudacorus*
Asclepias	*Kniphofia*
Aurinia	*Ligularia*
Caltha	*Lilium* species
Chrysanthemum morifolium	*Lupinus* species
Chrysanthemum parthenium	*Lysimachia*
Coreopsis	*Oenothera*
Digitalis	*Opuntia*
Doronicum	*Physalis*
Euphorbia	*Primula polyanthus*
Gaillardia	*Rudbeckia*
Geum	*Trollius*
Helianthemum	*Viola cornuta*

Opposite page: Here, yellow bearded iris is used to make a bold splash of color at Old Westbury Gardens, on Long Island.

Above: A red-hot poker plant and white shasta daisies are perfect companions in this sunny island bed.

Below: Yellow coreopsis and scarlet red cardinal flowers help to create an "old-fashioned" look in this Colonial garden at Pennsbury Manor, near Philadelphia, Pennsylvania.

PERENNIAL FLOWERING GUIDE

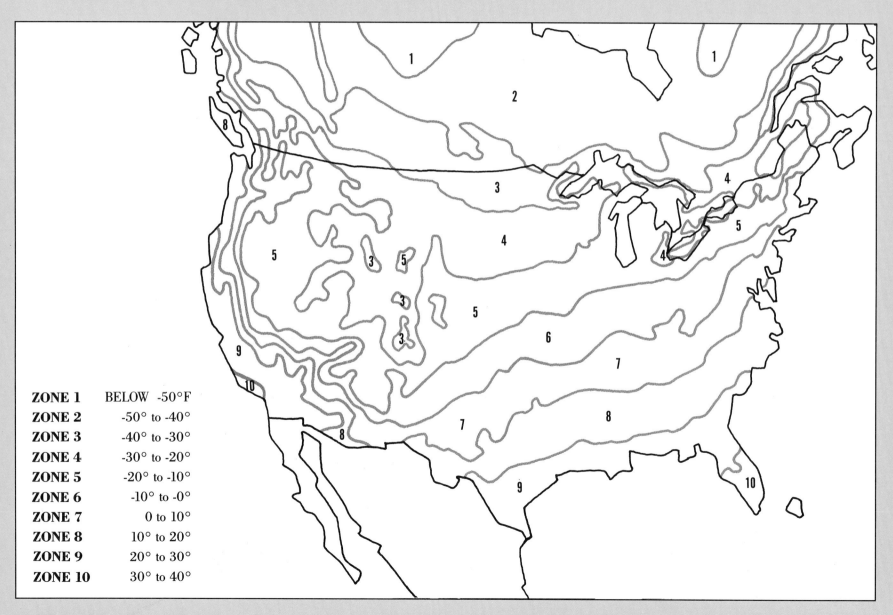

ZONE 1	BELOW -50°F
ZONE 2	-50° to -40°
ZONE 3	-40° to -30°
ZONE 4	-30° to -20°
ZONE 5	-20° to -10°
ZONE 6	-10° to -0°
ZONE 7	0 to 10°
ZONE 8	10° to 20°
ZONE 9	20° to 30°
ZONE 10	30° to 40°

PERENNIAL FLOWERING GUIDE

	January	February	March	April	May	June	July	August	September	October	November	December
Acanthus mollis (Bear's breach)							■					
Achillea filipendulina (Yarrow)						■						
Aegopodium podagravia (Bishop's weed)					■	■	■	■	■			
Ajuga reptans (Bluebugle)					■							
Alcea rosea (Hollyhock)								■				
Alchemilla mollis (Lady's mantle)						■						
Amsonia tabernaemontana (Bluestar)					■							
Anchusa azurea (Italian bugloss)						■						
Anemone x *hybrida* (Japanese Anemone)									■			
Anemone pulsatilla (Pasqueflower)				■								
Anthemis tinctoria (Golden Marguerite)						■						
Aquilegia hybrids (Columbine)					■							
Arabis caucasica (Rock-cress)				■								
Armeria maritima (Common Thrift)				■								
Artemisia ludoviciana (Silver King)					■	■	■	■	■			
Arum italicum (Italian Arum)							■	■				
Asclepias tuberosa (Butterfly Milkweed)						■						
Aster novae-angliae (Michaelmas Daisy)						■	■	■	■	■		
Astilbe x *arendsii* (False Spirea)						■	■					
Aubrieta deltoide (Flower Rock-Cress)				■								
Aurinia saxatilis (Perennial Alyssum)				■								
Baptisia australis (Blue wild Indigo)					■							
Bergenia cordifolia (Heartleaf Bergenia)			■									

		January	February	March	April	May	June	July	August	September	October	November	December
Caltha palustris	(Marsh-marigold)				▓								
Campanula percisifolia	(Willow-leaf Bellflower)						▓						
Catananche caerulea	(Cupid's-dart)							▓					
Centranthus ruber	(Red Valerian)						▓						
Cerastium tomentosum	(Snow-in-summer)					▓							
Chrysanthemum x *morifolium*	(Cushion Mum)									▓	▓		
Chrysanthemum parthenium	(Feverfew)												
Chrysanthemum x *superbum*	(Shasta Daisy)							▓					
Cimicifuga racemosa	(Snakeroot)							▓	▓				
Coreopsis lanceolata	(Lance-leaf Coreopsis)												
Delphinium elatum	(English Delphinum)												
Dianthus plumarius	(Cottage Pinks)					▓							
Dicentra spectabilis	(Japanese Bleeding-heart)					▓							
Digitalis purpurea	(English Foxglove)						▓						
Doronicum caucasicum	(Dogbane)					▓							
Echinacea purpurea	(Purple Coneflower)							▓	▓				
Echinops ritro	(Small Globe-thistle)						▓						
Erigeron hybrids	(Fleabane)					▓	▓						
Eryngium giganteum	(Sea-holly)						▓						
Eupatorium coelestinum	(Perennial Ageratum)								▓				
Euphorbia epithymoides	(Cushion Spurge)						▓						
Gaillardia x *grandiflora*	(Blanket-flower)							▓					
Geranium himaleyense	(Blue Cranesbill)						▓						

		January	February	March	April	May	June	July	August	September	October	November	December
Geum chiloense	(Chilean Avens)					▓							
Gypsophila paniculata	(Baby's-breath)							▓	▓				
Helianthemum nummularium	(Rock Rose)								▓	▓			
Helenium autumnale	(Sneezeweed)									▓			
Helianthus x *multifloras*	(Perrennial Sunflower)									▓			
Heliopsis helianthoides	(False Sunflower)								▓				
Helleborus niger	(Christmas-rose)			▓	▓								
Hemerocallis hybrids	(Daylily)						▓	▓					
Heucherea sanguinea	(Coral-bells)					▓							
Hibiscus moscheutos	(Rose mallow)								▓	▓	▓		
Hosta seiboldiana	(Plantain-lily)							▓	▓	▓	▓		
Iberis sempervivens	(Perennial Candytuft)				▓								
Iris germanica	(Bearded Iris)					▓	▓						
Iris sibirica	(Siberian Iris)							▓					
Kniphofia uvaria	(Red-hot poker)							▓					
Lathyrus latifolius	(Perennial Sweet Pea)								▓				
Lavandula angustifolia	(English Lavender)							▓	▓	▓			
Liatris spicata	(Gayfeather)								▓				
Ligularia x *prezewalskii*	(Rocket Ligularia)								▓				
Lilium lancifolium	(Tiger Lilies)									▓			
Linum perenne	(Blue Flax)					▓	▓						
Liriope muscari	(Lily-turf)					▓	▓	▓	▓	▓			
Lobelia cardinalis	(Scarlet Lobelia)								▓				

		January	February	March	April	May	June	July	August	September	October	November	December
Lupinus hybrids	(Russell Lupine)					X	X						
Lychnis chalcedonica	(Maltese Cross)						X						
Lysimachia punctata	(Yellow Loosestrife)						X						
Lythrum salicaria	(Purple Loosestrife)								X				
Monarda didyma	(Bee-balm)							X	X				
Myosotis scarpioides	(Forget-me-not)				X	X							
Nepeta mussinii	(Ornamental Catmint)						X						
Oenothera tetragona	(Sundrop)							X					
Opuntia humifusa	(Hardy Prickly-pear)						X						
Paeonia officinalis	(Herbaceous Peony)					X							
Paeonia suffruticosa	(Tree Peony)					X	X						
Papaver orientale	(Oriental Poppy)						X						
Perovskia atripicifolia	(Russian Sage)								X				
Phlox paniculata	(Summer Phlox)							X					
Phlox subulata	(Moss-pinks)					X							
Physostegia virginiana	(Obedient Plant)								X	X			
Platycodon grandiflorus	(Balloon flower)						X	X	X				
Physalis alkekengi	(Chinese lantern)								X	X	X		
Polemonium reptans	(Jacob's-ladder)					X							
Polygonum bistorta	(Knotweed)						X						
Pyrethrum roseum	(Painted Daisy)						X						
Primula japonica	(Japanese Primrose)					X							
Primula x *polyantha*	(Polyanthus Primrose)				X								

		January	February	March	April	May	June	July	August	September	October	November	December
Rudbeckia fulgida	(Black-eyed Susan)							▓	▓				
Salvia x *superba*	(Violet Sage)							▓	▓				
Saponaria ocymoides	(Soapwort)					▓							
Scabiosa caucasica	(Pincushion Flower)							▓	▓				
Sedum spectabile	(Stonecrop)									▓			
Stokesia laevis	(Stoke's Aster)						▓						
Trollius europaeus	(Globeflower)				▓	▓							
Veronica longifolia	(Speedwell)					▓	▓						
Viola tricolor	(Johnny Jump-Up)				▓	▓							
Yucca filamentosa	(Spanish dagger)							▓					

SOURCES

PERENNIALS— UNIQUE AND RARE

ANDRE VIETTE NURSERY
Route 1, Box 16
Fisherville, VA 22939

KURT BLUENOL, INC.
2543 Hess Road
Fallston, MD 21047

BLUESTONE PERENNIALS
7211 Middle Ridge Road
Madison, OH 44057

CANYON CREEK NURSERY
3527 Dry Creek Road
Oroville, CA 95965
Catalog $1

CARROLL GARDENS
P.O. Box 310
Westminster, MD 21157

HEATHS & HEATHERS
Box 850
Elma, WA 98541

HOLBROOK FARM & NURSERY
Route 2, Box 223B
Fletcher, NC 28732

STALLINGS NURSERY
910 Encinitas Boulevard
Encinitas, CA 92024
Catalog $2

WAYSIDE GARDENS
Hodges, SC 29695–0001

WESTERN HILLS NURSERY
16250 Coleman Valley Road
Occidental, CA 95465
Plant list $2

WHITE FLOWER FARM
Litchfield, CT 06759
Catalog $5

WILDWOOD FARM
10300 Highway 12
Kenwood, CA 95452

YERBA BUENA NURSERY
19500 Skyline Bouleavrd
Woodside, CA 94062

Index of Botanical and Common Names